D1608700

Getting the Schools You Want

Getting the Schools You Want

A Step-by-Step Guide to Conducting Your Own Curriculum Management Audit

Kimberly Logan

CORWIN PRESS, INC.
A Sage Publications Company
Thousand Oaks, California

For information:

Corwin Press, Inc.
A Sage Publications Company
2455 Teller Road
Thousand Oaks, California 91320
E-mail: order@corwin.sagepub.com

SAGE Publications Ltd.
6 Bonhill Street
London EC2A 4PU
United Kingdom

SAGE Publications India Pvt. Ltd.
M-32 Market
Greater Kailash I
New Delhi 110 048 India

Printed in the United States of America

Library of Congress Cataloging-in-Publication Data

Logan, Kimberly
    Getting the schools you want : a step-by-step guide to conducting
your own curriculum management audit / Kimberly Logan.
        p.   cm.
    Includes bibliographical references.
    ISBN 0-8039-6544-3 (pbk. : acid-free paper). — ISBN 0-8039-6543-5
(cloth : acid-free paper)
    1. Curriculum evaluation—United States.   2. Educational
accountability—United States.   3. Education—United States—
Curricula—Standards.   4. School management and organization—
United States.   I. Title.
LB2822.75.L64   1997
374'.006—dc21
                                                                    97-4767

This book is printed on acid-free paper.

97 98 99 00 01 02 03 10 9 8 7 6 5 4 3 2 1

Production Editor: S. Marlene Head
Editorial Assistant: Kristen L. Green
Typesetter: Andrea D. Swanson
Cover Designer: Marcia R. Finlayson

Contents

List of Forms, Exhibits, and Sample Documents

Foreword

Like all superintendents, I want to get the most for the children in my schools. I want to increase their achievement levels in the academic areas and through activities that will enable them to be productive adults. I want them to learn in safe schools. And I want them to succeed in a positive climate with support from parents and teachers.

However, most of my day is spent dealing with the barriers that can keep these things from happening:

- Board members who want to know why an athletic field fence is still down
- A teachers' meeting to debate which math program to adopt
- A parent who believes that their child is being treated unfairly because of the child's skin color
- District test scores inaccurately related through the media
- A late bus
- A principal out ill
- A bomb threat

Each of these activities challenges the educational system by shifting energy away from the business of educating students. I looked for a new system that would enable me to ensure that board members could focus on policy, that students and teachers would have the materials they needed, that all students would be treated equitably, that test data would be used to support program improvement, and that everything would come together every day to maximize the school system's productivity. The curriculum management audit has provided me with that system.

Getting the Schools You Want is the key to getting the schools *we* want. Whether you read it to prepare for an outside audit or to do a self-examination, you will find it valuable. It is easy to follow, the forms are clear and usable, and you can work at your own pace. And whether you choose to examine one standard from the audit system, or all five, you will have the documents you need to guide your school and district to immediate as well as long-term improvement.

GEORGE H. BLOCH, ED.D.
Executive Board Member
American Association of School Administrators
Superintendent, Madera Unified School District
Madera, California

Preface

The curriculum management audit is changing my former district. They are moving from unfocused, unproductive chaos to rational, systemic improvement. The mission is all-important: it guides them as they increase student achievement, provide safe schools, and promote positive school climates. The board has adopted comprehensive student learning expectations for every grade and every subject. The educational services division is rewriting every curriculum guide to support these expectations. Teachers and administrators are receiving training in the critical areas of the instructional focus: literacy, making a successful transition from primary language to English, and test wiseness. The assessment system is being put in place. Information about demographics and progress on each element of the mission is being used to make decisions about how to allocate resources. All aspects of the district's operation are being affected by adherence to the principles of the audit.

Having seen the power of the curriculum management audit in my own district, I am enthusiastic about the potential it has to provide a lifeline to other districts that are working to improve. The audit standards are the same regardless of the size, location, or history of the district. It can be used regardless of the tenure of the superintendent, the size of the district office staff, or any other characteristic. It will provide the district with findings, recommendations, and the insight to make meaningful change. This book offers a step-by-step guide to school improvement with a focus on conducting the internal audit.

The first four chapters provide background information about the audit. Chapter 1 expands on the use of the audit to support systematic change. It provides a process for determining readiness to undertake the process and offers reasons districts have undertaken the curriculum management audit. Chapter 2 defines what the audit is and is not. Chapters 3 and 4 delineate the principles and key concepts used in the audit process.

Chapters 5 through 9 present each of the five standards. Each chapter includes information about the questions that the audit seeks to answer, gives theoretical background needed to elicit facts, provides forms that can be directly copied and used in the audit report, gives sample findings from recently completed audits, and lists the data sources predominantly used.

Chapter 10 details the process of turning the facts gathered for each standard into findings and recommendations. Chapter 11 examines the organization of an audit and addresses the options of using an external team or an internal staff person. Chapter 12 ends the book with a glimpse into how a quality curriculum management system can hold a promise for the future.

The curriculum management audit is the work of Dr. Fenwick English. He developed the standards in the late 1970s while working for the Big Eight accounting firm then known as Peat, Marwick, Mitchell, and Co. Through work with numerous districts, he refined the standards and the processes used to audit them. Every aspect of the audit process is a result of his energy, his insight, and his commitment to quality education. His text, *Curriculum Auditing* (1988), is a scholarly guide to the tenets of the audit.

This book is for all educators faced with the need to produce results. Follow the guide and you will find yourself in a new world of success.

Acknowledgments

Fenwick English, where have you been all my life? Like countless others, I have spent years trying to improve schools. I've been battered by trying to make learning relevant, seeking to reform, rushing to restructure—and always ended up in about the same place, until now. Dr. English has developed a process that cannot help but improve a school. He has been generous enough to share this work with others so that fundamental change can affect learning for students from every walk of life. On behalf of all the students who will live better lives because of school improvement, thank you.

I also wish to thank Larry Frase, who made the curriculum management audit real in my life. From the initial training to the support for this book, you have provided insight, encouragement, compassion, and expertise. He has allowed me the flexibility to adapt the tools he gave me. His book, *The Curriculum Management Audit: Improving School Quality* (1995, Technomic), coauthored with Fenwick English and William Poston, is an invaluable guide.

Thanks to George Bloch who encouraged me to conduct an internal audit and whose district leadership has enabled us to embrace the mission. Thanks also to the Madera Unified School District Governing Board, an exceptional group of caring trustees who have withstood the findings and pursued the recommendations: Buz Boberg, Judy Crafton, Betty Finley, Joe Flores, Bob Garibay, Louise Houlding, and Barbara Roach. Thanks to my other daily faces: Jill Marmolejo, Adrienne Peters, and Pam Mendoza for steadfast support.

And thanks always to my daughter, Polly, who occupied herself while Mom was at the computer and to my husband, Rod, who keeps everything going.

KIMBERLY LOGAN
Ukiah Unified School District, California

About the Author

Kimberly Logan is superintendent of Ukiah Unified School District. She was previously the assistant superintendent for assessment and administrative services for Madera Unified School District. She has served as a school site and central office administrator in both traditional and alternative school settings at all grade levels. She has taught intermediate school, high school, adult school, and college English and social studies. Her public school and private sector experience spans more than 20 years.

She received her undergraduate and master's degrees from California State University at Bakersfield and her doctorate in educational leadership from the University of La Verne. She has conducted research into the forces that drive school change. She has presented sessions on the curriculum management audit in a variety of forums, including the national conference of the American Association of School Administrators.

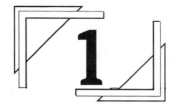

The Challenge to Change

Americans have become increasingly disappointed in the product of public education. They are alarmed by the number of school dropouts, the inadequate preparation of disengaged students, low morale among teachers, and the country's economic vulnerability. They want high-achieving students to surpass world-class standards. They want low-achieving students to reach higher standards. They want all students to become productive wage earners and healthy family members. They demand educational improvement complete with rigorous assessment and financial accountability.

Many of them want it to be done in the way that television depicts education of the 1950s. While Ozzie gets ready for work and Harriet arises from twin beds to provide breakfast, children are cheerfully brushing their teeth and tucking in their shirts. They gather their lunch boxes and head off to a classroom in which Miss Dove sternly checks for dirt under their fingernails before they are seated. Filmstrips will unveil the mysteries of the scientific world, multiplication tables will be mastered by third graders, and sentence diagramming will ensure that every student masters grammar.

Districts throughout the country are struggling to live up to their community's expectations about the quality of schools. As a result of the call for successful reform in the education system, educators are making numerous attempts at planned educational change. They bring in consultants. They reform. They restructure. They engage in a nearly endless cycle of adopting and abandoning initiatives. They transfer, reassign, and retrain teachers. They fire principals and superintendents in a continuous search for leaders with better results. They raise salaries and reduce class size. Then they hunker down and defend their quality by saying: "It isn't our fault—kids are so unprepared. We do the best we can but how can we possibly succeed with them?"

What the Critics Say

American schools have been thought to be in need of major change for quite some time. Criticisms and solutions have been offered by those involved with research, those who work in the system, diverse facets of the public at large, and a growing number of disenchanted employers. Educational researchers and practitioners have long exhorted schools to address their failures. R. G. Des Dixon (1994), an educational analyst, draws a dramatic analogy when he compares the school to an organism that "remains forever alive on life-support systems, even though it is brain dead." The late Albert Shanker (1990), who described public education as being on the edge of disaster, wrote,

> Our persistent educational crisis shows that we've reached the limits of the traditional model of education. Given our present and foreseeable demographic, economic, social, and educational circumstances, we can expect neither greater efficiency nor more equity from our education system. That statement is dramatic, but it also seems obvious. After all, there seems to be widespread agreement that we must do things differently in our schools. (p. 345)

Researcher Denis Doyle modifies the support of public education he announced in the first edition of *Winning the Brain Race: A Bold Plan to Make Our Schools Competitive.* In an article based on the revised edition of the book he coauthored with David Kearns, he supports the challenge public schools will face from the private sector. Doyle (1992) puts educators on notice when he writes,

> It is still disappointing to see how slow the pace of change is. Neither educators nor the public have forced the pace of reform and restructuring. Both have avoided that painful task. (p. 513)

And Keith Ferrell (1992) further addresses the issue:

> Perhaps no crisis more directly affects the direction and future of our society than the crisis of public education. Our schools are deteriorating, good teachers are abandoning the profession in lemming numbers, students perceive little value in the subjects they're

taught, officials of other nations openly mock our educational standards and institutions. (p. 8)

Consequently, communities throughout the nation continue to demand
answers to the same essential questions.

> There are so many people, plans, reports, rules, reviews, and policies
> in the district. Why can't the district control itself?
>
> Kids are graduating from high school unable to read their own diploma,
> much less balance a checkbook or earn a decent living. What are
> these students supposed to be learning?
>
> Teachers seem to teach whatever they like. Students learn different
> things at different schools even though they are in the same grade.
> The worse the student, the more likely that he or she will get a new
> teacher. Doesn't the district's left hand know what its right hand is
> doing?
>
> Test scores for the district are horrible. Teachers offer myriad reasons.
> Principals shrug and ask, "What can you expect? These kids' back-
> grounds aren't as good as those in the rest of the country." What do
> we need to do to improve our schools?
>
> We aren't getting our money's worth from schools. They are endless
> money pits that make excuses about why they can't do better. How
> much money will it take to produce a quality education for all
> children?

From the publication of *A Nation at Risk* (National Commission on
Excellence in Education, 1983) to the articles on school restructuring that
appear in journals daily, there is mounting evidence that schools are failing
to keep pace with community expectations. The stakes of such failings are
high: voter-rejected bonds, legislated voucher schools, dropouts and graduates unprepared to meet higher standards, and loss of local control—to
name but a few. There is little doubt that schools must work.

How Auditing Answers the Challenge

Auditing is the process of providing an objective, structured review of
something worthy of examination. An audit is both the process and the
written report that results from this examination. It is most typically
thought of in terms of financial audits, in which a qualified individual
studies the content of financial records and the process of their preparation.
It can be done by an outsider who is thought to be free from the constraints
of implementing recommendations. It can be done by an insider who is
expected to care about the quality with which the findings are developed.
Or it can be done by both with the internal auditor conducting a self-
examination that is subsequently verified or refuted by the findings of an

external auditor. Regardless of who conducts the audit, it is expected to represent an honest examination according to an agreed-upon structure.

In auditing, this structure is based on standards. Each standard represents what is thought to be best or ideal about an element being examined. In financial audits, these standards have been voted upon by the members of the American Institute of Certified Public Accountants and are known as generally accepted accounting principles (GAAPs). GAAPs provide a consistent way to find the facts and offer recommendations. These standards help the certified public accountant arrive at conclusions based on a review of documents, interviews with staff, and observations.

The Curriculum Management Audit

In the educational domain, the standards of the curriculum management audit represent the best thinking about the organizational aspects of the instructional program. The audit establishes five standards to which all schools should be held related to control, objectives, connectivity and equity, assessment, and productivity. It provides a guide to efficient planning, a vehicle to communicate with staff and the community, and a process for making real changes in student achievement.

Standards are used to assess the difference between the ideal and the real. This difference is generally stated as a finding that provides clear information about what the situation is and how it differs from what would be in a best-case scenario. Findings then lead to recommendations about what should be done to bridge this gap.

The auditing process was initiated in 1979 by Dr. Fenwick English in conjunction with the accounting firm of Peat, Marwick, Mitchell, and Co. Through the process spelled out in his book *Curriculum Auditing* (1988), a handful of districts (some 250 nationwide over 10-plus years) have brought outsiders into their districts to conduct an audit of their curriculum management. Much like financial auditing, these program auditors review documents, interview staff and students, and make visits to school sites to assess what is happening. They provide the district with findings and recommendations about how to improve the quality of their instructional program.

Increasing Interest in Auditing

Many state legislative bodies are now concerned with the accountability of the districts within their states. Although elected officials in the past were primarily interested in financial accountability, today many of them are pursuing legislation that will require an audit of program quality that greatly exceeds the parameters of existing accreditation and federal review processes.

Similarly, some school districts are pursuing auditing programs as a way of responding to community criticism. They hope that a systematic, public review will demonstrate two things: that they know what they need to do to improve and that they are committed to such improvement.

The factors of community scrutiny, fiscal crisis, dissatisfaction with the preparation of graduates for the workplace, lack of proven strategies for "fixing schools," and others combine to create a dilemma about how to proceed. Relevance movements of the 1970s, reform movements of the 1980s, and restructuring movements of the 1990s have not produced the desired changes. Schools are seen as floundering with no cogent plan for controlling the quality of education. The curriculum management audit provides such a plan.

Are You Ready for an Audit?

Despite external pressure to improve, many districts are reluctant to engage in in-depth scrutiny, whether internal or external. They fear that their warts will be revealed and that honest examination may cost employees their jobs. Therefore, before establishing such a time-consuming and demanding process, it is important to be sure that the district is, in fact, committed to undertaking the audit and to following through on the recommendations.

What follows is a two-part survey process to assess district readiness. Planning Form 1.1 is used to identify the staff members who will be affected by conducting the audit. The auditor can then determine who needs to be informed and who needs to be more actively involved in planning the audit process. Planning Form 1.2 is used to determine readiness. It will yield best results when it is completed by staff members who represent various aspects of the district's operation. Depending on the size of the district, such members may include the superintendent; the division administrators for business, educational services, and human resources; department heads within educational services; principals; teacher union representatives; site and district staff responsible for testing; and parent leaders. Using the two forms together, the district can assess its readiness and identify all staff members who need to be included in planning how the audit will be undertaken.

Once the staff members who are most likely to be affected by the audit have been identified, they can be involved in determining the district's readiness for an audit. This is important for two reasons. First, it gives staff an opportunity to discuss the potential for the audit. This ensures that they are aware of what will be done and gets information from them that will help the audit be successful. Second, it gives the key staff members an

(text continues on page 8)

Planning Form 1.1

On Whom Will Conducting the Audit Have an Impact?

Directions: Write the name of each staff member beside his or her area of responsibility. Put a check on the line to the left if the audit is likely to have an effect on that individual.

_____ Assessment   _____

_____ Board of education _____

_____ Business operations _____

_____ Communication   _____

_____ Community relations _____

_____ Curriculum   _____

_____ Educational services _____

_____ Facilities   _____

_____ Food services   _____

_____ Human resources   _____

_____ New-teacher support _____

_____ School site staff   _____

_____ Special projects   _____

_____ Staff development   _____

_____ Superintendent   _____

_____ Transportation   _____

_____ Union representative _____

_____ Other: _____

Planning Form 1.2

Are You Ready for an Audit?

Directions: Read each question below. Circle the number that best represents your view.

Question	1 = No 3 = Maybe 5 = Yes				
1. Has an audit been requested by any external party (e.g., the state department, a federal agency, a judge) or internal staff (e.g., board, superintendent, legal counsel)?	1	2	3	4	5
2. Is the community concerned about any of the following: a. How the district spends its money? b. How well prepared graduates are? c. How students are treated? d. How students do on standardized tests?	1 1 1 1	2 2 2 2	3 3 3 3	4 4 4 4	5 5 5 5
3. Are teachers concerned about any of the following: a. Knowing what they are supposed to teach? b. Having the materials they need to do their best? c. Having access to quality staff development? d. How the district's money is spent?	1 1 1 1	2 2 2 2	3 3 3 3	4 4 4 4	5 5 5 5
4. Is there a district commitment to change and risk taking?	1	2	3	4	5
5. Is there evidence that the district is interested in genuine improvement?	1	2	3	4	5

Open-ended: What other evidence do you have that the district is or is not ready for an audit?

opportunity to state their opinions and to let their opposition or support for an audit be known. Planning Form 1.2 should be completed by as many of the key staff members as possible.

There is no magical number that will indicate whether a district is ready for an audit. Many factors influence readiness; however, the higher the score, the greater the readiness. Needless to say, a board president can command that an audit be done at any point! But addressing those areas in which the scores are low may enable a district to increase its readiness in these areas now and avoid problems in the future.

Why Audit?

The curriculum management audit provides a district with a tremendous amount of information that can be used by many staff members to increase student achievement. The concepts of the audit can

- Affect transportation routes
- Change lunch schedules
- Define new orientation activities for teachers
- Gain community support
- Get grants
- Guide curriculum development
- Increase use of technology
- Justify additional staff
- Modify facilities
- Transform personnel evaluation

English (1988) identifies the element of risk taking that underscores readiness for an audit. At this time, no district has had only positive findings on a comprehensive audit of curriculum management; in fact, most districts have findings that define issues of concern that seriously challenge curricular quality. The staff and the community must be prepared for findings that show systemic problems that have historically kept students from achieving. The plan to audit is likely to be initiated when a new superintendent assumes the position or when the superintendent has spent 3 to 4 years addressing pressing issues and now needs a rational plan to effect new curricular change. But ideally it should occur at a time that is politically calm so that teachers can value the results, the district can implement the recommendations, and the results can be used to build support for the district's program.

Discussion Questions

1. What are the biggest challenges to change facing your district? What needs to be done to successfully confront these challenges?

2. Besides the factors listed in Planning Form 1.2, what other criteria might indicate readiness to audit in your district?

3. What experiences has your district had with audits? How do those affected generally respond to such self-examination?

4. What can you do to increase a staff's comfort with the idea of an audit?

5. How will the staff and community perceive the audit?

What the Audit Is and Is Not

One might expect a curriculum management audit to include a review of documents such as curriculum guides. One might expect it to require classroom observations of teachers. But where do such things as job descriptions for the director of transportation or a copy of the school lunch schedule fit in?

The curriculum management audit was developed to provide school districts with a tool to effect districtwide improvements. Financial audits have long been used to help institutions improve their fiscal control and related processes. Likewise, the curriculum management audit can be used to help districts improve quality control of their instructional program.

The audit is designed to determine the extent to which elected officials and professional staff have provided their district with a sound, valid operating system of curriculum management. This system is based on board-adopted policies. Its purpose is to enable the district to make maximum use of its resources so that students can be productive.

The audit is based on the notion of data corroboration known as triangulation. Documents, interviews, and site visits are used to gather information needed to arrive at findings. These findings and related recommendations are presented in a final written report, also referred to as the audit. The audit process is used to determine the extent to which a district is meeting its goals and objectives. It is intensive, and it is focused.

This focus sets parameters that exclude some things from review. The curriculum management audit does not examine district operations that are not related to one of the five audit standards. For example, the purchasing processes are not audited unless there is evidence that materials are not being provided to the classroom and, as a consequence, students are going without the supplies needed to meet instructional objectives. Support services such as custodial, maintenance, food service, business, and transportation are part of the audit only if concerns related to their role in supporting the instructional program arise.

The primary business of a school district is teaching, learning, and curriculum. The audit focuses on gathering data about the status of these activities. These data enable the auditor to arrive at findings. The findings are presented as a single sentence heading and are supported with narrative explanations. Many findings also include charts, lists, graphs, or summary sheets that provide additional support or detail. They do not usually include single incidents unless that single incident is so critical as to require specific noting.

The curriculum management audit is not designed to get people fired. Auditors have found that an individual's performance may suffer because of an inadequate curriculum management system. For example, a principal who is perceived as being a weak instructional leader may not be supported by a system with a clear instructional focus; consequently, the principal is not sure how to lead. Clear job descriptions, board-adopted policies, written curriculum guides, and a strong assessment program have probably saved more jobs than they have lost.

The Typical Outline

Curriculum management audits follow a fairly generic outline detailed in Exhibit 2.1.1.

This format supports successful two-way communication. The auditor is able to provide information about what the audit is, how it is conducted, and what was found. The audited district is able to understand the context of the audit, what was found, and what needs to be done to support school improvement. The audit sets a very high standard—five of them, in fact.

Discussion Questions

1. Is it appropriate to audit the art of teaching?
2. What are some examples of times when you felt unfairly judged because you were not well-informed or trained?
3. How might support services positively or negatively affect the district's mission?
4. How can a generic audit outline meet the needs of districts as diverse as those in your region?

Exhibit 2.1.1

Curriculum Management Audit Outline

I. **INTRODUCTION**   Information about when, where, and by whom the curriculum management audit was conducted and, if appropriate, how the audit came to be requested

    A. Background

       1. The community   A description of the community or communities in which the district resides, including pertinent factors such as square mileage, population, ethnic makeup, history, economy, employment statistics, median income, private schools, higher education

       2. The school district   History since established, growth trends, size, ethnic makeup, number and type of schools, enrollment, percentage of free and reduced lunches, specially funded programs, financial status

    B. Scope of work   An explanation of the curriculum management audit

II. **METHODOLOGY**

    A. The curriculum management   Information about curricular quality control; audit model   see Chapter 4

    B. Standards for auditors   Information about audit principles; see Chapter 3

    C. Data sources   Information about triangulation; see Chapter 3

    D. Standards for the audit   Information about the five standards; see Chapters 5–9

III. **FINDINGS**

    A. Standard 1—The school system is able to demonstrate its control of resources, programs, and personnel. (See Chapter 5.)

       1. What the auditors expected to find
       2. What the auditors found   An overview of findings to follow
       3. Finding 1.1   Information about board policies
       4. Finding 1.2   Information about long-range planning
       5. Finding 1.3   Information about the organizational structure
       6. Finding 1.4   Information about job descriptions
       7. Finding 1.5   Information about personnel evaluations
       8. Other findings   Information about any other control issues

B. Standard 2—The school system has established clear and valid objectives for students. (See Chapter 6.)
1. What the auditors expected to find
2. What the auditors found   An overview of findings to follow
3. Finding 2.1   Information about scope of curriculum
4. Finding 2.2   Information about adequacy of curriculum
5. Finding 2.3   Information about use of curriculum
6. Finding 2.4   Information about curriculum structure
7. Other findings   Information about any other objectives issues

C. Standard 3—The school system demonstrates internal connectivity and rational equity in its program development and implementation. (See Chapter 7.)
1. What the auditors expected to find
2. What the auditors found   An overview of findings to follow
3. Finding 3.1   Information about linkages
4. Finding 3.2   Information about curriculum monitoring
5. Finding 3.3   Information about staff development
6. Finding 3.4   Information about teaching quality
7. Finding 3.5   Information about resource allocation
8. Finding 3.6   Information about decision making
9. Finding 3.7   Information about equity
10. Finding 3.8   Information about any other connectivity and equity issues

D. Standard 4—The school system uses the results from system-designed and/or -adopted assessments to adjust, improve, or terminate ineffective practices or programs. (See Chapter 8.)
1. What the auditors expected to find
2. What the auditors found   An overview of findings to follow
3. Finding 4.1   Information about scope of assessment
4. Finding 4.2   Information about assessment results
5. Finding 4.3   Information about use of assessment
6. Finding 4.4   Information about data management plan
7. Other findings   Information about any other assessment issues

E. Standard 5—The school system has improved productivity. (See Chapter 9.)
1. What the auditors expected to find
2. What the auditors found   An overview of findings to follow
3. Finding 5.1   Information about facilities
4. Finding 5.2   Information about budget
5. Finding 5.3   Information about climate
6. Finding 5.4   Information about promising practices
7. Other findings   Information about any other productivity issues

IV. **RECOMMENDATIONS**   Suggestions for improvement (see Chapter 11)

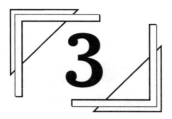

Role of the Auditor

Although most curriculum management audits are conducted by experts outside of the system being audited, they can also be conducted by district employees. Regardless of whether or not the auditor works in the system, English (1988) has identified seven fundamental principles that the auditor must understand and to which he or she must adhere.

Technical Expertise

Imagine yourself assessing the competence of a genetic engineer conducting an experiment. Or a train engineer programming the route to be taken. With training, you could probably do either well. Without training, you could probably do neither.

Although everyone seems to fancy themselves an expert about education, presumably because they attended school, the truth is that systematic analysis of a school system is a complicated business. It requires an understanding of how school works at the classroom, building, district office, and community levels. The auditor must have technical expertise to understand and evaluate what he or she is seeing and hearing at each of these levels.

The Principle of Independence

The external auditor cannot have any vested interest in the livelihood of the employees of the district nor can he or she expect to benefit materially from participation in the district after the audit recommendations have been received. The internal auditor must be in a position to be able to state findings and recommendations without fear of retribution.

The Principle of Objectivity

The auditor must be able to substantiate every finding with clear evidence that will withstand the scrutiny of others. The data used to support the findings must be derived from documents, interviews, and firsthand observation of sites. It is not sufficient to be told secondhand that something is true. All findings must be backed up by multiple sources of data.

The Principle of Consistency

To conduct a curriculum management audit, the auditor must use the appropriate methodology and processes to assess the five standards for control, objectives, connectivity and equity, assessment, and productivity. Audited school systems are not compared with one another. However, they are compared to these five standards. The auditor may choose not to undertake all five standards simultaneously, but for those that are evaluated, the methodology and processes of the previous audits are the accepted ones.

The Principle of Materiality

Although every effort has been made to support the principle of consistency, each district is unique. The principle of materiality allows the auditor the option of selecting the specific areas on which to focus and to identify the findings most critical given the status of the district. The auditor's role is to help the system improve, expand, terminate, or reconfigure its various function to ensure maximum productivity. It is the auditor's responsibility to identify those areas that most need to be brought to the district's attention. Each district's setting—state regulations and local policies—will have a unique impact on the audit. Auditors are also affected by the level of openness and trust and by the prevalent needs of the student body.

The Principle of Full Disclosure

Confidentiality of information obtained through interviews is respected. However, the auditor is expected to reveal all pertinent information unless to do so would compromise an individual's or a group's identity.

It is important to accurately disclose data obtained from individuals. This is especially true when not all of the members of a certain group or class were interviewed. If the auditor speaks to 10 teachers out of 500 and 6 of them say they have never seen a curriculum guide, it is not accurate to report that the majority of teachers have never seen a curriculum guide. The auditor has no way of knowing through those 10 interviews whether the other 490 teachers have seen one. Additional information must be gathered before reaching such a conclusion.

The auditor uses descriptive terms to quantify information, as follows:

Descriptive Term	General Range Within the Group or Class Interviewed
Some, or a few	Between two and five people determined by the overall size of the group
Many	More than 30% and less than a majority
A majority	No less than 50% and up to 75%
Most	75–89%
Nearly all	90–99%
All, or everyone	100%

Adapted from audits sponsored by American Association of School Administrators' National Curriculum Audit Center.

No Artificial Balance

Most readers of audits are struck by the lack of positive statements. Outside program reviewers, such as accreditation teams and compliance reviews, typically include a number of commendations. In all but the worst situations, the number of commendations is likely to equal the number of recommendations.

However, this is not the case in the curriculum management audit. There is no manufactured balance between good and bad. All audit statements are intended to be useful to the district and therefore such contrived compliments as "The bulletin boards are especially attractive" and "The children look nice in their uniforms" undermine the auditor's intent.

Discussion Questions

1. What are the comparative strengths and weaknesses of using an external auditor or an internal auditor?
2. Which principles may present the most difficulty in your system?
3. What are some findings that an auditor in your district might not pursue at this time? Why?

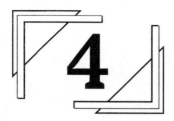

Key Concepts in the Audit

In the medical profession, certain standard courses of treatment have been developed for numerous diseases. These treatments are known as protocols. Everyone who has a comparable disease will receive the same protocol with some adjustments for the needs of the individual. The curriculum management audit is similar. English (1988) has designed a protocol in which every audit follows a comparable process with some adjustments for the unique nature of each district. Regardless of size, location, program, community, or budget, the concepts behind each audit are the same.

Standards

All auditors organize their activity around five standards. These standards define what a school system should do if it is to demonstrate the highest quality control. When these standards have been attained, the district can be assured that every opportunity to be productive is being maximized. Although the auditor does not have to audit all five at one time, the comprehensive audit includes the following (English, 1988):

1. **The Control Standard**—The school district demonstrates its control of resources, programs, and personnel.

2. **The Objectives Standard**—The school district has established clear and valid objectives for students.
3. **The Connectivity and Equity Standard**—The school district has demonstrated internal consistency and rational equity in its program development and implementation.
4. **The Assessment Standard**—The school district has used the results of district-designed or -adopted assessments to adjust, improve, or terminate ineffective practices or programs.
5. **The Productivity Standard**—The school district has improved its productivity.

Collectively, these five standards provide a model for the highest goals a school district can reach. Success in each area increases the likelihood that students will be learning at optimum levels.

Curriculum Alignment

The foundation of the audit is the premise that schools are systems and, as such, can control their quality. To attain quality, three elements of the system must be in place (English, 1992; Frase, English, & Poston, 1995).

The first element is the written curriculum, which must include the mission, goals, objectives, and standards that are expected. The written plan is found in the curriculum guides and in the district's various planning documents.

The second element is the taught curriculum—the actual instruction that occurs in every classroom every day. In a system with good quality control, the teaching is directly related to the written curriculum. The district provides all teachers with sufficient guidance to know what they are supposed to do, when to do it, and what resources are available. It provides this in such a way that teachers have a foundation from which to effectively meet the needs of each student in the classroom.

The final element is the tested curriculum, which provides feedback about how students are doing relative to the district's expectations (criterion-referenced testing) and relative to other students in the country (norm-referenced testing).

In a district without a high level of quality control, some of what is written will be taught and many things that are taught will not have been written. As a consequence, testing of students may have no relationship to either what is written or what is taught, and student's test scores, therefore, will not favorably impress the community. The teachers will tell their neighbors that it is no big surprise—explaining how "That exam does not test what I teach."

These three elements—the written, taught, and tested curriculum—overlap in a district with a high level of quality control. Most of what is written will be taught; what is taught will make up what is tested; what is tested will provide information to revise what is taught and how it is tested.

Bringing these three elements together is known as curriculum alignment. A fundamental principle of the curriculum management audit is the belief that the more a curriculum is aligned, the greater will be the quality of the educational program. An aligned curriculum will cause

- Test scores to increase
- Teacher satisfaction to improve
- Resources to be optimally directed
- Staff development to meet real needs
- Technology to support instruction
- The school district to be more productive

Triangulation

The focus of much of the curriculum management audit is on curriculum alignment. Tremendous amounts of data are gathered so that conclusions, known as findings, can be established. Anyone who has played the children's game Gossip—in which a secret statement is whispered to a player and subsequently whispered one by one to each participant, with the last player's version compared with the original message—knows that there is no single source of information upon which one can rely. Auditors recognize this and look for information that comes from three different primary sources.

The first source is documents. Written evidence used by auditors includes board policies, meeting minutes, curriculum guides, scope and sequence charts, job descriptions, organizational charts, budgets, class schedules, district phone directories, parent club meeting agendas, salary schedules, site floor plans, inventories—the list can go on for pages for most comprehensive audits.

The second source is interviews. The auditor has formal interviews with many key people including board members, the superintendent, central office staff, site administrators, teachers, support staff, parents, and community members. The auditor also talks with a cross section of people who represent the interests of the business office, educational services, and the human resources department. In addition, he or she talks to those who have axes to grind, those who are happy with their positions, those who are new, and those who are veterans. Finally, the auditor may have informal interviews with secretaries, custodians, cafeteria workers, and security staff.

Auditors have adopted two critical conventions regarding interviews. In the first convention, all interviews begin with the same question: What are the strengths and weaknesses of this district? This gives interviewees an opportunity to talk about something they know well, to share the things of which they are proud, and to identify the most serious concerns. Some interviews will deviate from the original plan, and focus instead on following up on the answer to this one question. The second convention is to avoid questions that can be answered with a yes or a no. Interview questions are generally open-ended, which provides much richer information for the auditor.

The third source for data is on-site visits. The auditor visits every classroom in every site in the district. Many of these visits last less than a minute. Some are longer when the teacher is available for an interview. Some visits are accompanied by the principal and some are unaccompanied. The auditor is focused on the staff, the students, and the facilities. For auditors who use cameras to document their observations, this is an especially rich source of data.

Documents, interviews, and on-site visits combine to provide what the auditor calls *triangulation*. These three sources of data must be used to corroborate the findings. The auditor's work begins when a single data source reveals something of importance, but it does not end until the two other sources have been explored for information that supports or refutes the first.

Discussion Questions

1. Which standards seem most critical to the situation your district is currently facing?
2. What impact would curriculum alignment have on students in your district? On teachers?
3. What techniques for interviewing have you found most helpful? Least helpful?
4. Why might auditors believe that triangulation has kept them from ever producing a false finding?

The Control Standard

Standard 1: The school district is able to demonstrate its control of resources, programs, and personnel.

When greeting others, some people say "Hi." Some wonder, "How are you doing?" Some ask, "Everything under control?" The latter question is usually greeted with laughter, snickers, and shoulder shrugs. Many of us struggle to maintain the appearance of control. The notion that we would actually *be* in control stretches our imagination.

Audit Standard 1 acknowledges that school districts should, in fact, be in control of themselves. Districts need to be organized in such a way as to control resources including money, time, equipment, and materials. Districts should have control over the number and implementation of their programs, both special and regular. They should also design controls to ensure that the work of those on its payroll can be directed to meet their districtwide needs. The goal of these controls is not to constrict resources, programs, or personnel; rather, it is to be certain that these are effectively connected to the district's central mission. Quality control is fundamental to the well-managed school system.

What the Auditor Expects to Find

The curriculum management auditor looks for answers to three questions in Standard 1:

1. Are there written documents that provide for control?
2. What is the quality of the written documents?
3. What is the use of the written documents?

Three specific types of documents are examined: board policies, planning documents, and organizational charts.

Board Policies

The curriculum management auditor looks for curriculum, curriculum policies, and procedures that have been adopted by the governing board. A clear set of policies should explain how curriculum will be managed and contain enough detail to know who is accountable for each aspect of its management.

To provide the staff with sufficient guidance, these policies should provide answers to 20 questions.

1. **Is the written, taught, and tested curriculum to be aligned?** The board should expect teachers to use the written curriculum that they have adopted to guide their choice of teaching strategies as well as their selection of materials. They should also expect that teacher and district testing will be based on the written curriculum. By ensuring that instructors teach and test the written curriculum, the board can maximize the opportunity for students to achieve.

2. **What philosophical approach is taken to curriculum?** Educators teach and test according to the philosophical approach built into the written curriculum. The board should clarify its philosophy about learning to support the teachers' instruction. There are three typical organizational philosophies:

A standards-based philosophy, in which there is understanding before beginning a unit or lesson about what must be accomplished and at what achievement level

A mastery- or competency-based philosophy, in which there is agreement prior to instruction about what must be accomplished before moving to the next lesson or skill, and agreement about how such accomplishment will be demonstrated

A continuous progress philosophy, in which there is ongoing measurement that supports the development of skills over a period of time

3. **Does the board adopt all curriculum?** It is the responsibility of the governing board to adopt all curriculum. This does not mean that they play an active role in researching or writing curriculum. It does mean, however, that they should provide the resources needed for the staff to develop curriculum. The board should be familiar with the key issues facing the curriculum developers, such as the critical elements of frameworks, current research, and community interest. They should officially adopt the written curriculum after providing the community and staff with an opportunity to become familiar with its contents.

4. **Are there staff members who are accountable for curriculum management?** The board should be very clear about who is responsible for developing, implementing, and monitoring curriculum. In very small districts, this responsibility tends to fall on the superintendent and principal and may be supported by a county or regional office. In larger districts, the central office is likely to have specialized staff, such as an assistant superintendent for education, a director of curriculum and instruction, and subject area specialists. Regardless of district size, the board must be clear about who is expected to perform that role.

5. **Does the district have a strategic plan or other board-adopted documents to guide its long-term development?** The curriculum management auditor is not only interested in the district's past and present. The district's planning documents will provide insight into what the district has identified as future areas of concern and the remedies they are considering. A well-done strategic plan will also define the environment in which curriculum management will be done. Other documents—such as grant applications, accreditation reports, and compliance reviews—will also detail the district's plans.

6. **Is there to be written curriculum for all subject areas?** The board should provide a clear, nonnegotiable mandate that there is to be a written curriculum for every subject area and, in fact, for every course that is taught. The alignment of written, taught, and tested curriculum is fundamental to the notion of control. Without a board-approved written curriculum for everything that is taught, this control is compromised. There should be no course too urgent or so transitory that time cannot be taken to write a quality curriculum guide.

7. **Is the curriculum to be periodically reviewed?** Curriculum reflects what is most important for students to know or be able to do. The benchmark about what is most important changes as the knowledge base, the job market, the community's expectations, and students' proficiency levels change over time. It is important that curriculum be reviewed no less than every 4 years and that this review be done in conjunction with textbook adoption cycles.

8. **Are textbooks and key resources adopted by the board?** Textbooks and the myriad resources available present a unique challenge to the board. When the curriculum is originally adopted, it is likely to be organized according to a text specifically mandated by the state. This text will probably be in use for the duration of the curriculum (usually 5–10 years). In the meantime, the teacher will attend staff development training about the subject and how to teach it, he or she will become aware of other materials, and new technologies will emerge. The board needs to determine how much control it wishes to exert over the adoption of these resources.

Many boards have taken the position that the textbook will be approved as part of the curriculum adoption and that supplemental resources will be selected as appropriate by the teacher. Although this is reasonable, it is also somewhat risky. There is probably no area more likely to prompt unhappy community visitors to the board meeting podium than the misuse of videotapes, novels on the supplemental reading list, and simulation games.

9. **Is some curriculum content emphasized more than others?** Four areas of the curriculum have long been considered critical—so critical that they are known as "core" curriculum:

Language arts
Mathematics
Social studies
Science

Most districts have also recognized the critical nature of the arts and physical education, although these tend to be cut when budgets get slashed. Now, however, some very specific areas of content are being given highest priority—among them, reading at grade level and use of technological tools. Because there are so many different topics that fill the school year, it is important for the board to identify those elements that are most critical. The teacher can then plan instructional time and strategies to support the board's plan.

10. **Is it expected that curriculum from one grade or level to another will be predictable, articulated to higher and lower levels, and coordinated across programs?** Lessons that build upon each other into units that build upon each other enable the curriculum to be predictable. This supports instruction at a lower level by providing a foundation for learning at the next level, which promotes articulation. Coordination of curriculum ensures that the experience a student has in one class at one grade in one school is comparable to that of another student in a similar situation elsewhere in the district.

These three elements—predictability, articulation, and coordination—enable curriculum implementation to be efficient, support sharing of resources, and are a catalyst to good planning. They are critical to the efficiency of a quality curriculum continuum.

11. **Will staff be trained in the delivery of the curriculum?** No written guide will make learning happen. Only quality teaching can do that. Teachers, whether they are veterans or novices, need support in understanding what is expected of them when a new curriculum is released. They also need to share their experiences as they work through the curriculum. They will benefit from opportunities to exchange strategies that worked and resources that did not. The staff must be trained initially and throughout implementation. They must have opportunities to reflect on and revise the curriculum.

12. **Is quality curriculum delivery expected?** It is a given that not all teachers will deliver all curriculum equally well. However, it is the board's right to clearly state its requirement that quality instruction is expected. This lays the groundwork for the staff development plan, for staff evaluations, and for the district to have control over the learning experiences provided to its students.

13. **How will curriculum delivery be monitored?** Board policy should identify who is responsible for monitoring the curriculum and how such monitoring is to be done. Typically, site administrators accept this responsibility. They may review lesson plans, make regular classroom visits, quiz students, or undertake myriad strategies to assure themselves that when the teacher's door is closed, every student is being given an opportunity to learn.

14. **Is equitable access to curriculum expected?** All children can learn, and they can learn at high levels. The board needs to provide a clearly communicated statement that all students will have the chance to learn well regardless of their gender, ethnicity, age, socioeconomic status, family background, or any other factor.

15. **Is assessment expected?** Board policies typically provide for the written and taught curriculum. Less frequently, however, they make a statement about the tested curriculum. The board should establish its plan for norm-referenced and criterion-referenced testing within the confines of external legislation and in order to meet the needs of local decision makers. The board policy may also explain how students can be formally exempted from assessment.

16. **Will data be used to determine program and curriculum effectiveness and efficiency?** Once the board has established that assessment is expected, it is ready to state how data will be used to increase student achievement. Whether the data emanates from individual, disaggregated

scores or is building- and district-summary information, expectations about its eventual use need to be clearly set out before any research design is developed.

In smaller districts, the data might be used by the school site administrators. In larger districts, a department of research and evaluation may be responsible for interpretation and reporting. The board needs to guide whatever approach is suitable to the district with an expectation that assessment matters and with information about how results will be used.

17. **Will the board receive reports about program effectiveness?** The days when testing was solely the business of the school or program are long gone. Parents, businesspeople, and legislators are all interested in the evidence of a school's success. The board policy should stipulate before assessment how and when it expects to receive evaluation reports. Whether they are corporate-style annual reports or school report cards, the board should be clear about how progress on its mission is to be measured and when it is to be reported.

18. **Will resources be tied to curriculum priorities?** Having the written, taught, and tested curriculum aligned is fundamental to the budget process. The board needs to recognize that district expenditures must be evaluated in terms of the curriculum priorities it has established. If the instructional focus is reading for all students by third grade, then second-grade teachers should not be shocked to get their request for playground equipment rejected. If assessment is expected, funds should be budgeted for test administration. All of the district's discretionary funds should be reviewed in terms of the curriculum including materials, equipment, supplies, contracts, repairs, staffing, and staff development. General funds as well as special project funds should be tied to the curriculum priorities.

19. **Will curriculum priorities be supported with resources?** Just as the board supports curriculum with staff training, it needs to support it with resources. These may include new or refurbished facilities for science or the arts, manipulatives for math, magnetic letters for language arts—the list is endless. Every resource should be tied to the curriculum according to a well-thought-out, long-term plan.

20. **Will the board make decisions about increasing student learning on the basis of data?** The board should be very clear about what decisions will be made using data. As soon as such a statement is made, two serious concerns will arise.

First, staff will want to know exactly what data are going to be used and how can they make themselves look as good as possible when the results come in.

Second, staff will want to know what the consequences are if the data do not "look good." Will people lose their jobs? Can administrators be reassigned? Will instructional support staff be eliminated? The board needs to consider the use of data to identify a school that is not performing up to expectations and develop a policy that addresses these issues.

In writing the policies that answer these questions, the board should capitalize on its ability to provide for local control. This requires an understanding of the community's history, related policies, employment contracts, and other local issues. The policies need to provide direction, whereas the administrative regulations can provide related description and detail. The board should provide a focus that current and subsequent boards can follow until the policy is institutionalized. All policies should be distributed to all staff members who have need of them. Information about the board policies is recorded in Exhibits 5.1.1 and 5.1.2.

Exhibit 5.1.1 is a list of each board policy that was reviewed. It provides the number or code used by the district and the general topic of the policy. It is important to list each policy so that a clear record of the review is established. A staff member might contend that the results of the board policy analysis are incomplete. If the policies have been listed, a quick review of its contents will determine if the auditor has, in fact, not reviewed a policy that is germane to the analysis.

Exhibit 5.1.2 is a form for recording the answers to the 20 questions asked about the board policies. After each question, the auditor lists the number or letter code of the policies reviewed and puts a check mark if the policy is adequate to answer the question. The auditor does not write the answer, but merely indicates whether the policy provides sufficient information for the district to answer the question.

The auditor is also interested in determining the percentage of questions that have adequate answers. One of the findings will be based on this information. The formula for this statement is

_____ of the 20 questions, or _____ percent, were adequately answered.
_____ of the 20 questions, or _____ percent, were inadequately answered.

Planning Documents

Once the board has established direction in policy, the staff can develop its implementation plan. The curriculum management auditor assesses 10 components of the district's planning documents. The following 10 questions guide that assessment.

1. **Is there a statement about the mission of the district that clearly defines the purpose for which the district exists?** The mission is a short statement of the general purpose of the district. It can be easily memorized and is the focus of planning, spending, learning, communicating, and

Standard 1—Exhibit 5.1.1

Curriculum Management Policies Reviewed

Policy Code	Description/Topic

Standard 1—Exhibit 5.1.2

Curriculum Management Policy Assessment

Each question below was audited. The board policies that were reviewed to answer the question are identified by code (number or abbreviated title). If the policies provide sufficient direction to answer the question, there is a check in the "OK" box. If there was no policy, the box is left blank.

Question	Board Policy/Policies CODE	OK
1. Is the written, taught, and tested curriculum to be aligned?		
2. What philosophical approach is taken to curriculum (e.g., is it based on continuous progress, performance, etc.)?		
3. Does the board adopt all curriculum?		
4. Are there staff members who are accountable for curriculum management?		
5. Does the district have a strategic plan or other board-adopted documents to guide its long-term development?		
6. Is there to be written curriculum for all subject areas?		
7. Is the curriculum to be periodically reviewed?		
8. Are textbooks and key resources adopted by the board?		
9. Is some curriculum content emphasized more than others?		
10. Is it expected that curriculum from one grade or level to another will be		
a. Predictable?		
b. Articulated to higher and lower levels?		
c. Coordinated across programs?		
11. Will staff be trained in the delivery of the curriculum?		
12. Is quality curriculum delivery expected?		
13. How will curriculum delivery be monitored?		
14. Is equitable access to curriculum expected?		
15. Is assessment expected?		
16. Will data be used to determine program and curriculum effectiveness and efficiency?		
17. Will the board receive reports about program effectiveness?		
18. Will resources be tied to curriculum priorities?		
19. Will curriculum priorities be supported with resources (e.g., facilities, materials, etc.)?		
20. Will the board make decisions about increasing student learning on the basis of data?		

undertaking all of the activities of the school day. The mission is direct and presents a philosophy of improvement toward an enticing future.

2. Is there a critical analysis that provides data about the district and the environment in which it operates? School planning used to be a process in which a site staff came together and answered the question What shall we do this year? Most likely, that answer was based on a commitment to continue the activities of the past and take on a few new ones. Which activities those would be came from general agreement about what seemed appropriate.

School planning today is an entirely different process. It involves many more people and replaces untested agreement with consensus. Which activities will be added, however, is still often a result of general agreement about what seems appropriate.

Interest in critical analysis is changing that. More and more, people are looking at data to make their decisions. These data include test scores, climate surveys, local newspaper reports, accreditation reports, compliance reviews, student petitions, and as many other sources as there are students and staff. Critical analysis includes an inward look at data from the school; it includes an external examination of the workplace, the community, and the future. The critical analysis component of a plan defines the status of the district and forecasts its future.

3. Are there assumptions that predict the events and conditions likely to have an impact on the district in the future? Nothing is as certain as change. But good planners recognize the need to be public about the assumptions upon which their plans for change are founded. These assumptions may be demographic projections. They may be economic predictions. They may be time-honored beliefs about how schools will operate. Regardless of the source, assumptions need to be shared so that they can be monitored.

4. Are the key goals stated and grouped so that they can be effectively communicated and managed? Most plans have more goals than the staff can handle at any one time. That does not make the last item on the list less worthy but it does have a lesser chance of being achieved. By stating and grouping goals people can see the connections. This will support coordination of resources so that as one goal is being pursued, it can be done in a way that supports as many other goals as possible.

5. Do the objectives support the goals by providing measurable improvement statements with time limits? Once the general goals are agreed upon, objectives can be written. These objectives must be clear so that there is minimal room for misinterpretation. They must be measurable so that progress can be assessed and necessary changes made. They must further the goal according to an agreed-upon time frame. Finally, they must state the desired improvements in such a way that everyone can see what role they will play.

6. **Is there evaluation for every objective?** An objective that is not evaluated is not likely to be accomplished. When the plan is prepared, each objective must include information about who will be evaluated, and how and when.

7. **Is there an action plan for each objective?** The evaluation accounts for one element of the action plan. Information about activities, timelines, and resources are other elements critical to accomplishing the objective. The written action plan must clearly delineate what will be done, when each activity will begin and end, and what resources will be required. The more an action plan can be perceived as "marching orders," the less likely it is that critical pieces will be forgotten or misunderstood.

8. **Is there a system for monitoring the status of activities, the results, and the reporting mechanism?** Those who delegate effectively know that "out of sight" cannot be "out of mind." Once the action plan has been agreed upon, every aspect of its implementation must be monitored. There are several reasons for this. Without mandatory progress checks, activities may not be initiated as intended. Coordination will not occur. Most important, corrections that are needed will go unnoticed until it is too late.

The planning system should identify an individual responsible for overall plan coordination. Progress reporting and checkpoints should be agreed upon, posted, and adhered to. Many districts find that routine reports to the governing board both keeps them on track and supports the ongoing communication that is essential to a successful audit.

9. **Are all key stakeholders represented in the plan development?** Districts cannot control those things that blindside them. If all those who are likely to have an impact on their operation are brought into the planning process, blindsiding is less likely to occur. Some key stakeholders for school districts include business leaders, elected officials, government employees, graduates, local college staff, parents, preschool owners, retirees, school neighbors, site and central office staff, social service agencies, students, and vendors. The district's strategic planning will include representatives from many of these groups. Action plan development is likely to include many others according to the goal.

10. **Are all key documents in the district linked to the plan?** Strategic plans can be little more than SPOTS (Strategic Plans On Top Shelves). After hundreds of hours involving dozens of people and several dead trees, many such documents find themselves relegated to the "When we get time we'll try some of this" file.

The strategic plan that is a guiding document, however, will be readily available. It will be seen in many different locations. Most important, it will be referred to in other documents such as grant applications, school improvement plans, the district's annual report, and other public papers.

Exhibit 5.2.1 is used to record the curriculum management planning documents that were analyzed. It provides a place to list each document that was provided by the district to the auditor as a strategic plan or other significant planning document.

Exhibit 5.2.2 is used to record the answers to the 10 questions about the quality of the planning documents. The name of the document(s) is listed and a check mark is used to indicate that the document provides adequate direction.

Organizational Charts

The organizational chart—also known as a table of organization or T/O—has come to be an increasingly important part of the curriculum management audit. This document depicts the key positions in the district and demonstrates their relationship to each other. A well-made chart will show employees who their supervisor is, which departments are related, whose duties are comparable to their own, and how the various district departments and divisions relate to each other.

There are numerous types of useful organizational charts. Many are made of boxes and lines with names and titles of critical management positions. Increasingly, organizational charts contain rings, pyramids, or other models of key functions that depict interrelationships. Many show the community or governing board at the top whereas some show students as the driving organizational force and depict the administrative staff at the bottom. Some documents that are presented as organizational charts are, in fact, flowcharts that show how decisions get made.

Regardless of how the chart is formatted, the analysis focuses on the principles of sound organizational management. It is clear to any educator that one person can supervise only so many others effectively and that employees should not have lots of different supervisors. It is also clear that the written chart should follow certain principles of presentation to be clear and to accurately reflect how the district is organized. These principles form the basis of the six-question analysis of organizational management.

The curriculum management audit examines the following six aspects of the organizational chart (English, 1988).

1. **Span of Control.** The audit standard expects that no manager will directly supervise more than 12 employees. This span of control defines how far an administrator can stretch to provide adequate oversight of the employee and his or her productivity. It is not uncommon for superintendents to have

(text continues on page 36)

Standard 1—Exhibit 5.2.1

Planning Documents Reviewed

Planning Document Description/Topic	Code	Date Document Was Prepared

Standard 1—Exhibit 5.2.2

Planning Documents Assessment

Each question below was audited. The planning documents that were reviewed to answer the question are identified by code (number or abbreviated title). If the documents provide sufficient direction to answer the question, there is a check in the "OK" box.

Question	*Planning Documents*	
	CODE	*OK*
1. Is there a statement about the MISSION of the district that clearly defines the purpose for which the district exists?		
2. Is there a CRITICAL ANALYSIS that provides data about the district and the environment in which it operates?		
3. Are there ASSUMPTIONS that predict the events and conditions likely to have an impact on the district in the future?		
4. Are the key GOALS stated and grouped so that they can be effectively communicated and managed?		
5. Do the OBJECTIVES support the goals by providing measurable improvement statements with time limits?		
6. Is there EVALUATION for every objective with information about who will be evaluated, and how and when?		
7. Is there an ACTION PLAN for each objective with information about activities, timelines, and resources?		
8. Is there a system for MONITORING the status of activities, the results, and the reporting mechanism?		
9. Are all key STAKEHOLDERS represented in the plan development?		
10. Are all key documents in the district LINKED to the plan?		

a span that greatly exceeds this, particularly in midsized districts if they have retained supervision for all principals as well as division or department heads. It is also not uncommon for classified managers to be the sole manager of programs with dozens or even hundreds of employees.

Being common, however, does not make it a good practice. Effective daily supervision is compromised by having more employees than can be routinely met and observed.

2. **Chain of Command.** Many districts recognize that they have a chain of command when they draw their organizational chart. They find employees who have lines connecting them to so many different departments that the chart becomes confusing. The audit standard requires that no employee have more than one supervisor. Although this is exceedingly difficult in small districts where the differentiation of duties is challenged by the available resources, it is still a goal. When an employee does have more than one supervisor, it is important that the challenges to quality control be anticipated.

3. **Logical Grouping of Functions.** Some organizational charts seem to be a random depiction of functions. Transportation, purchasing services, and staff development may be shown in the same area. A usable organizational chart will have easily discerned groups of comparable services. Usually these will be organized by departments within such divisions as administrative services, educational services, and human resources.

4. **Separation of Line and Staff.** Districts have "line" employees. These are generally school site positions with direct responsibility for instruction and its day-to-day management. Line employees include principals, teachers, and instructional support staff. Districts also have "staff" employees. These are positions that provide services used by the line employees. Staff employees include central office staff and school-based support staff. The organizational chart will separate these two functions.

5. **Scalar Relationships.** One of the major challenges facing the person who creates the organizational chart for a complex district is to understand who does what and the relationship between one position and another. Sometimes, however, the bigger challenge is to depict those relationships on a single sheet of paper.

The organizational chart needs to show the relationships among departments and divisions. It also needs to do so in such a way that their comparative relationship to the superintendent is evident. Generally this means that assistant superintendents will appear on one line, directors on another, coordinators on another, and so forth. All staff whose names or titles appear on the same line should be comparable in scope of responsibility and authority, as well as in compensation.

6. **Full Inclusion.** The organizational chart will account for all of the functions of the district. This will show school site staff what services they can use.

Within administrative services, this is likely to include the following functions:

Accounting
Accounts payable/receivable
Assessment
Budgeting
Child nutrition
Communications
Community relations
Data processing
Facilities maintenance and operations
Legal counsel
Payroll
Planning
Print services
Purchasing
Research
Risk management
Technology
Transportation
Warehousing

Within educational services, this is likely to include the following functions:

Activities
Athletics
Curriculum (including subject areas and special needs)
Exceptional education
Grant development
Instruction
Special projects
Staff development
Student services

Within human resources, this is likely to include the following functions:

Administrative services
Certificated services
Classified services
Substitute services

At the school site, this is likely to include the following functions:

Principal
Assistant principal
Psychologist
Counselor
Teacher
Librarian
Certificated resource staff
Instructional aide
Nurse
Custodian
Activities and athletics staff
Mentor
Translator
Parent liaison
Speech therapist
Secretary
Clerk
Student helper
Department or grade supervisor and specialist

Exhibit 5.3.1 is used to record information about the analysis of the organizational chart. In general, only one chart format will be provided so a list of chart names is not needed. A check mark is used to indicate that the document provides adequate direction to answer the question about organizational management.

Job Descriptions

New employees are eager to see their job descriptions. Veteran employees are interested in their job descriptions when they sense change is imminent. Supervisors review them when they are dissatisfied with employee performance. Generally, all of them are looking for answers to four key questions.

1. **What qualifications is a person in this position supposed to have?** The job description should include a list of qualifications that is separate from the responsibilities. The list should identify expected experiences such as education, specialized training, and employment. It should also include abilities that are needed for the person to succeed in the position.

Standard 1—Exhibit 5.3.1

Organizational Chart Assessment

Each question below was audited. If the organizational chart provides sufficient direction to answer the question with a yes, there is a check in the "OK" box.

Question	*Organizational Chart* OK
1. Is the SPAN OF CONTROL sufficient to provide a full-time manager for at least every 12 employees under his or her supervision?	
2. In the CHAIN OF COMMAND, does every employee have just one supervisor?	
3. Is there LOGICAL GROUPING OF FUNCTIONS in which employees with similar responsibilities are together?	
4. Is there SEPARATION OF LINE AND STAFF that shows school positions distinct and apart from curriculum management positions?	
5. Do SCALAR RELATIONSHIPS depict positions at the same levels of responsibility, authority, and compensation in the same way?	
6. Is there FULL INCLUSION in which all staff members who support curriculum management are included on the chart?	

Adapted from audits sponsored by American Association of School Administrators' National Curriculum Audit Center.

2. **Who supervises them?** The title of the supervisor should be clearly stated. It usually is not appropriate to name the person since this is likely to change. However, the title should be included and when supervisory title changes occur, the job descriptions of those being supervised should be revised to reflect this change. For example, if the director of food services becomes the director of child nutrition, everyone supervised by this person should receive a revised job description that reflects this change.

In keeping with the organizational management principle that each employee has one supervisor, only one supervisory title should be included on a job description. The job description may include the employee unit in which the person is included (e.g., classified, certificated, administrative, or classified management).

3. **What, exactly, are they supposed to do?** Understanding what to do is critical to each employee's contribution to the organization. The general responsibilities and specific duties that are unique to the position should be clearly, unambiguously, and completely stated.

It generally is expected that each list of responsibilities will conclude with the statement "Other related duties as assigned." The use of the word *related* protects the employee from capricious assignments for which he or she may not be prepared. The phrase *as assigned* protects the employer from the employee who takes on responsibilities without asking and then submits a claim for working out of classification or becomes injured doing a task in an unsafe manner.

4. **How does their work fit in the district's curriculum?** The mission of the school district is controlled by its curriculum. Every job description should demonstrate the alignment between the position and the design and delivery of the instructional program. Phrases that the auditor can expect to see in the list of responsibilities include

Teaches [subject or grade]
Monitors instruction
Supports the classroom by . . .
Oversees curriculum
Evaluates teaching staff
Works with students

Each job listed on the organizational chart should have a job description. In this portion of the audit, the auditor lists each job on the chart on Exhibit 5.4.1. The date when the job description was adopted is also included. The adequacy of answers to each question is coded as follows:

Standard 1—Exhibit 5.4.1

Job Description Assessment

In column 1, each *job title* on the organizational chart is listed.
In column 2, the *date* the job description for that position was adopted is listed. A blank indicates that there is no job description for the position.
In column 3, the adequacy of information about *qualifications* has been rated.
In column 4, the adequacy of information about the *chain of command* has been rated.
In column 5, the adequacy of information about *job responsibilities* has been rated.
In column 6, the adequacy of information about *relationship to curriculum* has been rated.

Job Title	Date	Qualifications	Chain of Command	Job Responsibilities	Relationship to Curriculum

S = Strong   Clear statement was made including several or all
                    aspects of alignment, design, and delivery of
                    curriculum
A = Adequate   Clear statement was made but is weak in curriculum
                    quality control element
I = Inadequate   Statement was made but is missing basics of quality
                    control
M = Missing   No statement was made

Adapted from audits sponsored by American Association of School Administrators' National Curriculum Audit Center.

Certificated Personnel Evaluations

Teachers

The prevailing wisdom suggests that since teachers cannot be fired, a truce is to be called by administrators doing evaluations. Instead of accurate information about weaknesses, faint praise of strengths—however limited—is provided. The opportunity to improve teaching is sacrificed.

Teacher evaluations provide a district with control in three areas: establishment of standards of competence, fostering individual growth, and promoting school improvement. A good evaluation system provides teachers and administrators with a clear statement of what competence is, how it is measured, and where each individual is in the process of mastering each standard. Not only does it provide for communication about the standard, it lays the groundwork for each teacher to develop a plan for improvement, and it defines district resources needed to assist teachers in their growth. Meaningful staff evaluation ties individual teacher performance to staff development activities in accordance with school site curricular programs.

The critical component in the audit of teacher evaluation is the extent to which the process is productive. Hundreds of administrative hours are spent annually to evaluate teachers. A well-managed system will ensure results by providing the evaluated person with constructive feedback geared toward improving his or her performance.

In this portion of the audit, the auditor completes Exhibit 5.5.1 by listing all system documents used to audit the district's certificated personnel. The description focuses on the role each document plays in the evaluation system. The auditor will typically find

1. Board policies that provide the intent and purpose for evaluation
2. Contracts that detail the evaluation process to be used

Standard 1—Exhibit 5.5.1

Certificated Personnel Evaluation Documents Reviewed

Evaluation Document Name/Source	Purpose

3. Evaluation forms developed by the state or district that delineate the standards
4. State law that relates how evaluation is to be conducted

The auditor uses Exhibit 5.5.2 to assess actual teacher evaluations provided by the human resources office. The district must adhere to its policies and contractual obligations regarding anonymity. Regardless of what those may be, the auditor needs to review a random sample of approximately 15% of tenured teachers and nontenured teachers for the previous 2 years. Each evaluation is assessed as showing performance that is unsatisfactory, is satisfactory, exceeds expectations, or is clearly outstanding. The district terminology may be substituted for these phrases as long as they are comparable.

The exhibit graphically depicts the percentage of teachers who have been evaluated in each performance area. The graph will be created four times, each clearly labeled to show the school year in which the evaluations were administered for

a. Tenured teachers from the school year before last
b. Nontenured teachers from the school year before last
c. Tenured teachers from the last school year
d. Nontenured teachers from the last school year

As a result of the review of the random sample, classroom visits, and staff interviews, the auditor will be prepared to make a number of statements about the productivity of the teacher evaluation system. Typical statements include

Certificated personnel evaluation is nonproductive in providing constructive feedback that can be used to improve job performance.
The number of evaluations marked "unsatisfactory" was not reflective of the quality of teaching noted in classroom observations.
Most evaluation comments were not substantive (e.g., were not easily understood, did not pertain to critical aspects of the instructional practice, offered no specific suggestions for improvement).
Evaluation practice does not meet the criteria of state law and board policy.
Evaluation practice does not help teachers improve.
Some instructional practices did not meet reasonable expectations for quality, with such things as excessive use of work sheets, students sleeping, low-level cognitive activities, and student isolation from teachers being commonly observed.

Administrators

The auditor uses Exhibit 5.5.3 to assess actual administrator evaluations provided by the human resources office. Again, the district must adhere to

Standard 1—Exhibit 5.5.2

Distribution of Ratings for Random Sample (15%)

Tenured/Nontenured Teachers for School Year _____

The percentage of teachers rated Unsatisfactory is _____

The percentage of teachers rated Satisfactory is _____

The percentage of teachers rated Exceeds Expectations is _____

The percentage of teachers rated Clearly Outstanding is _____

%

50

45

40

35

30

25

20

15

10

5

0

Unsatisfactory   Satisfactory   Exceeds Expectations   Clearly Outstanding

Standard 1—Exhibit 5.5.3

Distribution of Ratings for Random Sample (15%)

Instructional/Noninstructional Administrators for School Year _____

The percentage of teachers rated Unsatisfactory is _____

The percentage of teachers rated Satisfactory is _____

The percentage of teachers rated Exceeds Expectations is _____

The percentage of teachers rated Clearly Outstanding is _____

%

50

45

40

35

30

25

20

15

10

5

0

    Unsatisfactory   Satisfactory   Exceeds Expectations   Clearly Outstanding its policies and contractual obligations regarding anonymity. The auditor needs to review a random sample of approximately 15% of instructional and noninstructional administrators for the previous 2 years charted in four exhibits. Instructional administrators are those considered to have primary responsibility for the design and delivery of curriculum—for instance, principals, directors of curriculum, and instructional supervisors. Noninstructional administrators include those who do not have curriculum as their primary responsibility—for instance, the business manager and director of transportation.

The exhibits provide information about each evaluation showing performance that is unsatisfactory, is satisfactory, exceeds expectations, or is clearly outstanding. Again, the district terminology may be substituted for these phrases as long as they are comparable.

The auditor will complete and label four exhibits:

a. Instructional administrators from the school year before last
b. Noninstructional administrators from the school year before last
c. Instructional administrators from the last school year
d. Noninstructional administrators from the last school year

As a result of the review of the random sample, classroom visits, and staff interviews, the auditor will be prepared to make a number of statements about the productivity of the administrative evaluation system. Typical statements include

Administrators receive inadequate feedback on their job performance.

Administrative evaluation fails to meet the requirements of board policy or state law.

Administrative evaluation is not sufficiently related to professional growth plans in the areas of _____. (Examples could include instructional monitoring, subject area expertise, classroom management, research about learning, conducting of performance appraisals, or design and delivery of instructional improvement plans.)

The number of evaluations required for an administrator to complete is inappropriate.

Instructional leadership skill varied among _____. (Examples could include grades, subjects, veteran administrators, or those who completed a specified training program.)

About the Findings

Board policies, strategic plans, organizational charts, job descriptions, and certificated personnel evaluations provide the focus for the audit of Standard 1. When this audit has been completed, the district will be able to develop improvement plans that improve control. A review of curriculum management audits completed in the last 2 years reveals a number of findings in common that are directly supported by the process provided in this chapter. Typical findings have included the following.

1.1 Board Policies

Board policies are inadequate to guide curriculum quality control.

Board policies provide a basic curriculum management framework but need additional development and refinement to ensure quality control.

Board policies lack clear organization, consistent coding and formatting, and legal documentation.

Many board policies are outdated and ineffectively implemented.

1.2 Planning Documents

No strategic plan or long-range plan exists.

Long-range planning is fragmented, inadequate, and ineffective.

Districtwide planning lacks coordination.

Planning is ineffective for directing system improvement.

The mission statement is neither reflective of the board's beliefs nor is it a true mission statement.

The strategic plan is widely accepted by staff but is not directly linked to improved student achievement.

1.3 Organizational Charts

The table of organization is inadequate to guide organizational productivity and efficiency.

The organizational chart does not match existing practice.

Central office administrative ratios exceed those recommended for quality control of instruction.

Organizational structure is inadequate to support the district's site-based initiatives.

1.4 Job Descriptions

Job descriptions exist but are inadequate to drive instructional improvement.

Job descriptions are outdated and do not match present responsibilities.

There are mismatches between some personnel job requirements and skills.

1.5 Certificated Personnel Evaluations

> Certificated personnel evaluation is nonproductive, instructional leadership training is inadequate, and the quality of instructional leadership practice varies.
>
> Instructional supervision and evaluation practices vary across the school system.
>
> Teacher evaluation reports do not effect instructional improvement through professional growth.
>
> Staff evaluation practices give teachers unduly high ratings.
>
> Teacher evaluation reports are inflated and of insufficient quality to effect instructional improvements.

Often, in the course of auditing the control standard, unanticipated findings will emerge. If these findings clearly have an impact on the district's control of resources, programs, and personnel, they need to be included. As with the above findings, statements that are unique to the district can only be included if they can be supported with evidence from a review of documents, interviews, and on-site visits; that is, they must be triangulated. Such Standard 1 findings from previously conducted audits include the following:

> Poor communications and improper board behaviors preclude optimal educational effectiveness.
>
> Negative relations exist among the board, the administration, and the staff, impairing readiness for improvement.
>
> The school system contributes unduly to internal conflicts for school trustees.
>
> The district trend toward site-based management has blurred the district focus on curriculum and instruction.
>
> Distrust impedes organizational control.
>
> Perceived changes at the governance and executive levels of the district have significantly different effects on staff and central office administration.
>
> Staff development is inadequate and ineffective in supporting district needs and priorities.

Preparing to Audit Standard 1

To audit this standard, you will need to gather the following documents:

> Statements of the district's mission, philosophy, beliefs, and expectations about learning
>
> The district's strategic plan and planning documents
>
> The district's curriculum and materials published about its curriculum

All board policies and administrative regulations related to making decisions about curriculum, including its evaluation, development, assessment, materials acquisition, and course construction

All board policies and administrative regulations related to making decisions about the budget, including budget development and monitoring

The district's organizational chart and job descriptions for all staff named in the organizational chart

A random sample of 15% of the tenured and nontenured teachers and the instructional and noninstructional administrative staff for the 2 most recently completed school years

The district's internal telephone directory with staff names, titles, and numbers

Make arrangements to interview the following:

- All current board members
- The superintendent
- Key central office staff responsible for curriculum management
- Key site staff responsible for curriculum, including the principal, curriculum director, resource teachers, and both new and veteran teachers
- Parents and students

You also need to develop a schedule to conduct school site visits.

Discussion Questions

1. What are some of the good and bad aspects of control?
2. What are the aspects of control in which specific stakeholders are most interested? Consider the governing board, students, parents, teachers, teacher unions, administrators, taxpayer associations, and legislators.
3. In your experience, what elements of a school system not presented here have an impact on control?
4. How would auditing this standard help guide a teacher to increased student achievement?
5. How could clear board control affect the classroom?

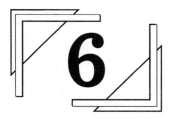

The Objectives Standard

Standard 2: The school system has established clear and valid objectives for students.

The agenda is set. The notices have gone out. The press is informed. There will be a series of meetings beginning next month with hundreds of staff and community representatives. Their task? To reach agreement about what students should know and be able to do before they graduate.

Sound familiar? Districts across the country have invested countless hours involving their staff and community in addressing this question. Some of these sessions have been productive. Others have led to community-wide strife and litigation. Either way, the district has been left with direction of some sort about what their community does or does not want.

Regardless of the number involved or their gender, educational background, or socioeconomic level, people pretty much want the same things for all students. People want students to

- Communicate clearly and properly, orally and in writing
- Know and apply the foundation skills of mathematics
- Understand and appreciate the history of America
- Understand and apply the basic principles of earth, physical, and life sciences

- Create and appreciate the arts
- Maintain physical fitness and mental health
- Be capable of lifelong learning, planning, problem solving, and decision making
- Be employable

These global statements become objectives around which graduation requirements, curriculum, and resources can be organized. English (1988) established Audit Standard 2, which confirms that a district with quality curriculum management has clear and valid objectives for all of its students to ensure successful instruction toward what the district believes to be the appropriate goals.

What the Auditor Expects to Find

The curriculum management auditor looks for answers to three questions in Standard 2:

1. Is there a written curriculum?
2. What is the quality of the written curriculum?
3. How is the written curriculum used?

The primary focus of this standard is on written curriculum guides. In some districts and at some grades these are called *courses of study* or *course guides*. They may be scope and sequence charts. They may be old or new. They may be slick and attractive or 10th-generation copies of teacher manuals. They may be lists of national reforms or local initiatives. Whatever form they take, this standard examines those written documents that guide the teacher in determining what to teach and how to teach it.

Curriculum Guide Scope

To provide the staff with sufficient direction, written curriculum guides should be available for every subject that is taught in the district. Without a written curriculum, the alignment upon which curriculum management is based cannot be sound. Teachers will not know what the board deems critical. They will not know what subject matter goals their school has. They will have a hard time discovering what resources are available at their school or in the community. They will be left with little more help than a page-by-page recitation of the textbook. Having written guides for each curriculum offered is the issue of scope.

To complete the audit for the scope of curriculum guides, the auditor completes Exhibit 6.1.1. This form provides for a listing of all curriculum areas or subjects taught in the district by grade level in column 1. The number of courses offered at different grade levels (i.e., elementary, middle, and high school levels) is entered into columns 2, 4, and 6. The number of written course guides provided by the district for each of those levels is listed in columns 3, 5, and 7. The total number of courses is in column 8 and the total of guides by course is in column 9. At the bottom, the auditor provides a total number of courses and guides by grade level and the percentage of courses covered by the written guides.

To have "adequate scope," a district must have written curriculum guides for at least 70% of the possible content areas. The percentage of guides by grade level is the number at the bottom of columns 3, 5, and 7. The total, on which district adequacy is judged, is the number at the bottom of column 9. Using this exhibit, the auditor will be able to provide specific information about the adequacy of curriculum guides by curriculum area and by grade level.

Curriculum Guide Quality

Establishing the scope of the written document is the first step in Standard 2. However, if the document is of little or no value, its availability is pointless. The Standard 2 auditor's next task is to assess every written guide for quality using the following five criteria.

1. **Clarity and Validity of Objectives.** Every curriculum guide should state the key objectives of the course. Each objective should include what is to be learned, when the objective will be introduced, how student progress in attaining the objective will be measured, and how much time is to be spent on the objective.

A typical guide will list the objectives sequentially. New teachers should be able to look at this listing and know what to teach first, second, and thereafter. They should also have guidance in pacing so that they will cover the objective in the depth expected but not lose focus and spend the entire course on the initial objective. The objective should also provide guidance about how to measure students' performance.

2. **Congruity to Testing and Evaluation.** The written curriculum is a tool in the board's accountability program. It needs to include guidance to teachers about how their students' progress will be measured and when. Each objective should indicate if measurement will be by teacher observation, standardized test, authentic performance, or some other assessment. It should include information about when to test so that the teacher can

Standard 2—Exhibit 6.1.1

Scope of Curriculum Guides by School Level and Curriculum Area

Column 1	2	3	4	5	6	7	8	9
	Elementary		Middle		High		Total	
Curriculum Area/Subject	# Courses	# Guides	# Courses	# Guides	# Courses	# Guides	# Courses	# Guides
Language Arts/ English								
Math								
Social Studies								
Science								
Fine Arts								
Physical Education/ Health								
Career Education								
Technology Education								
Electives/ Other:								
Total percentage								

plan time for instruction, initial assessment, reteaching or enrichment, and cumulative testing.

3. **Delineation of Skills, Knowledge, and Attitudes.** Some students are treated as if they had no exposure to a skill or topic being introduced. Others are treated as if they had total mastery of previous learning experiences. Rarely is either the case. The written guide needs to identify the prerequisite skills, knowledge, or attitudes that a student should possess before participating in a lesson. This may be minimal, such as expecting a student to pronounce each lowercase letter before reading a primer. It may be more complex, such as expecting the student to have previous writing and research skills before presenting a culminating project. Any prior skills, knowledge, or attitudes that a student needs to succeed with the new material should be identified.

4. **Delineation of Instructional Tools.** Teachers spend more than enough of their own money on classroom materials beyond the school budget. They do not need to spend excessive time reinventing the wheel as well. The written curriculum guide should provide specific information about available resources that are appropriate for every objective. Although this list may change over time, initially it should include the specific chapter or pages in a text, videotapes, software, on-line addresses, community resources, speaker contact information, games, manipulatives and other hands-on equipment, and any other instructional tool that is needed to support good first teaching, reteaching, enrichment, and assessment of the objectives. Information should be specific so that the novice teacher knows exactly what materials to use, when to use them, and how to access them.

5. **Clear Linkages to Classroom Use.** If the curriculum guide meets the first four criteria, it may be a powerful tool in assisting the teacher to provide quality instruction. If not, it may sit in a stack of untouched documents. If the guide provides clear linkage to instruction, it is more likely to be of use. The key linkage that is needed is through specific examples of how to reach the objectives. This may be detailed lesson plans. It may be annotated general suggestions. It may be pictures, floor plans, or quizzes. It does not need to be provided for every lesson, but the more specific the examples, the more guidance the teacher will have.

To analyze these five criteria, the auditor uses the Individual Record (Exhibit 6.2.1). This form is completed for each written guide that is assessed. In many districts, this will number several hundred. The form is for use by the auditor and does not appear in the final audit report.

To complete the Individual Record, the auditor will analyze each written guide in terms of the five criteria. Each criteria has a rating scale of 0 to 3. These ratings are totaled and the Individual Records are put in rating order from a high of 15 to a low of 0.

Standard 2—Exhibit 6.2.1

Curriculum Guide Criteria Assessment: Individual Record

Course _____ **Grade(s)** _____

Each of the five criteria below has been rated and assigned a number of points.

Criteria		Points
1. Clarity and Validity of Objectives		
No goals or objectives are included.	0	
Objectives are included but are vague.	1	
Objectives include tasks, skills, and/or concepts.	2	
Objectives include what, when, how, and how long.	3	
2. Congruity to Testing and Evaluation Process		
No evaluation approach is stated.	0	
Some evaluation approach is stated.	1	
Skills, knowledge, and concepts which will be assessed are stated.	2	
Evaluation approach is keyed to objective and district testing program.	3	
3. Delineation of the Essential Skills, Knowledge, and Attitude		
Required skills are not mentioned.	0	
General necessary prior experience is stated.	1	
General prior experience in specified grade or course level is stated by grade.	2	
Specific documented prerequisite or description of discrete skills and concepts required is stated by grade.	3	
4. Delineation of Major Instructional Tools		
Textbook or instructional tools are not mentioned.	0	
Basic texts or tools are named.	1	
Basic texts or tools and supplementary tools are named.	2	
All texts and tools are matched by objective.	3	
5. Clear Linkages for Classroom Use		
No links to instruction are provided.	0	
Overall, vague links to instruction are provided.	1	
General suggestions on approaching instruction are provided.	2	
Specific examples on how to approach key skills and concepts are provided.	3	

Adapted from audits sponsored by American Association of School Administrators' National Curriculum Audit Center and Frase et al., 1995, p. 144.

Once all of the curriculum guides have been analyzed, the information about them is transferred to and summarized in Exhibit 6.3.1—Rating and Rank of Curriculum Guides by Criteria. This provides a master list of every guide, the year it was published, the grades it covers, the number of pages in the document provided to the auditor, the individual criteria ratings, and the overall curriculum guide ranking. The guides are presented in rank order from highest points out of 15 possible to the lowest, with 0 possible.

On the last line of the last page of data, the auditor computes and adds the mean score for each criterion. This number is the total of all scores for the criterion divided by the number of guides. The mean guide ranking is also computed by totaling all of the rating scores and dividing by the number of guides.

The auditor then presents the mean rating by criterion in Exhibit 6.3.2. The auditor will also provide narrative analysis of the data to identify the range of total scores for the guides, the strongest criterion, and the weakest criterion.

Curriculum Guide Use

If the written guide is available and of the highest quality but is not used, it is still pointless. The curriculum management auditor will focus on interviews with teachers and site administrators to gather data related to curriculum guide use. Although every interview needs to be tailored to the person and the setting, the following questions will help guide the interviews.

Classroom Teachers

1. What are the key goals for your subject/grade? How do you know this?
2. How do you know or decide what to teach each year? Each day?
3. If you want to teach something for the first time or in a different way, how do you go about it?
4. How is the curriculum for your grade or subject monitored? How often do you see the person responsible for monitoring?
5. How do you know if what you are doing in class is okay with the board or your school?
6. How often do you refer to the written curriculum guide? For what reasons?
7. What would make your curriculum guide more valuable to you? To new teachers?
8. What assistance do you get in teaching your grade or subject?
9. How do you know if you are "on schedule" throughout the year?

(text continues on page 60)

Standard 2—Exhibit 6.3.1

Rating and Rank of Curriculum Guides by Criteria

Each curriculum guide has been audited. They are presented here, as ranked, from the highest score to the lowest.

Curriculum Guide Title	Date Published	Grade Level(s)	# of pages	Criteria					Audit Total
				1	2	3	4	5	
		Average							

Adapted from audits sponsored by American Association of School Administrators' National Curriculum Audit Center and Frase et al., 1995, p. 146.

Standard 2—Exhibit 6.3.2

Mean Rating of Curriculum Guides by Criterion

Criterion	Description	Mean Rating (Out of Possible 3.0)
1	Objectives	_____
2	Assessment	_____
3	Prerequisites	_____
4	Resources	_____
5	Strategies	_____

Adapted from audits sponsored by American Association of School Administrators' National Curriculum Audit Center.

Kimberly Logan, *Getting the Schools You Want.* Copyright © 1997 by Corwin Press, Inc.

10. How do you learn about resources that relate to what you are teaching?

Site Administrator

1. What are the key instructional goals for your school? How do you know this?
2. Who is responsible for monitoring curriculum at your school? What, specifically, do they do?
3. If your staff wants to teach something for the first time or in a different way, what do you need them to do?
4. How do you monitor the curriculum for your school? How often do you see the people you monitor?
5. How do you know if what you are doing in your school is okay with the board or your superintendent?
6. How often do you refer to the written curriculum guide? For what reasons?
7. What would make the curriculum guides more valuable to you? To new teachers?
8. What assistance do you get in curriculum monitoring at your school?
9. How do you know if your teachers are "on schedule" throughout the year?
10. What school efforts are under way now that promote quality teaching?

In addition to interviews, the auditor will want to visit with teachers in their classrooms. The auditor is looking for evidence of the degree to which the curriculum guide is used. Evidence would include such things as the curriculum guide on the desk or shelf, written objectives on the blackboard, resources organized by instructional topic, and lesson plans or tests keyed to the objectives in the guide.

It is also possible that such evidence will not be obviously arrayed. Probing may be needed before a judgment is reached: Is the curriculum guide filed away forever unopened or at the teacher's home office where it is referred to every night? Is this a novice teacher who has brought exceptional order by labeling all of the very few resources available or a veteran with a storage room of materials off campus? Is this curriculum being piloted or taught for the sixth time this year? Only by testing preliminary observations with specific questions or document reviews will the auditor be assured of an accurate finding.

Curriculum Management System Structure

The district may have written curriculum guides for all subjects. These guides may be of the highest quality. They may be used as the key to direct instruction. But if they are not supported with a system for design and delivery, these qualities will be short-lived.

The existence of the system will be found in the board policies, planning documents, organizational charts, job descriptions, and curriculum guides used in Standards 1 and 2. However, they will also be found in minutes from curriculum meetings, in budget allocations for curriculum development time, in conversations with staff, and in classroom observations. Specifically, the auditor is looking for evidence that there is a procedure for the design, development, and review of the curriculum. This includes information to answer eight fundamental questions.

1. Which subjects or grades are in which stages of design, implementation, review, and revision?
2. What is the schedule, scope, and procedure for review?
3. What are the procedures for establishing and revalidating goals and objectives?
4. How does testing and other assessment data affect the curriculum?
5. How can changes be made once the new curriculum has been implemented?
6. How can new resources be incorporated in the ongoing curriculum?
7. Do the staff members responsible for the curriculum speak knowledgeably about the elements of curriculum management?
8. Are new and special programs involved in the curriculum management structure in a manner that is comparable to traditional curricular areas?

Without sound answers to these questions, districts are likely to be in disarray. Teachers will often report: "We don't know what they want us to do." The atmosphere will be charged with frustration and insecurity resulting from concern about whether or not students are being prepared in accordance with the district's expectations. Without quality written curriculum guides, teachers cannot do their best work and students will not achieve the measurable goals that the community expects.

About the Findings

Curriculum guides and interviews provide the focus for the audit of Standard 2. When this audit has been completed, the district will be able to develop improvement plans that support the curriculum management system. A review of curriculum management audits completed in the last 2 years shows that findings related to scope, availability, and use are common to nearly all Standard 2 audits. Most audits also include a finding related to a fourth area: curriculum management system structure. The following sample findings show the range of information that the auditor can provide after completing the Standard 2 process.

2.1 Scope

The scope of the written curriculum is inadequate.
Nearly all curriculum offerings are not covered by curriculum guides.

2.2 Adequacy

The written curriculum guides are inadequate to guide instruction.
Curriculum guides lack elements to ensure clear instructional focus.
The curriculum guides are inadequate to guide _____. (Examples could include assessment, selection of resources, objectives, etc.)
The written curriculum is _____. (Examples could include descriptive terms or phrases such as *one-dimensional, inconsistently complete, inconsistently formatted, overloaded*, etc.)

2.3 Use

The use of curriculum guides is _____. (Examples could include descriptive terms or phrases such as *sporadic, inadequate to direct instruction in a specified grade or subject*, etc.)
Curriculum guides in program X are not used to guide instruction.

2.4 Curriculum Management System Structure

The curriculum management structure is inadequate to provide for quality design and delivery.
A cycle for curriculum development, review, and revision has not been established.
The curriculum management system is _____. (Examples could include descriptive terms or phrases such as *inconsistently implemented, lacking clear direction, unfocused, not well-defined*, etc.)
The curriculum management system of goals and objectives has not been adopted by the board.

Preparing to Audit Standard 2

To audit this standard, you will need to gather the following documents:

- All board policies and administrative regulations related to making decisions about curriculum, including its evaluation, development, assessment, materials acquisition, and course construction
- Minutes of board, central office, and school site meetings in which curriculum has been discussed
- Reports to and from governing bodies, accreditation organizations, government agencies, or others that pertain to what is expected of students
- Curriculum guides and courses of study
- Scope and sequence charts
- Curriculum planning documents, including course review and textbook adoption schedules
- School schedules listing the name of each course taught
- Staff and student handbooks

Make arrangements to interview the following:

- Key central office staff responsible for curriculum management
- Key site staff responsible for curriculum, including the principal, curriculum director, resource teachers, and both new and veteran teachers
- Subject-matter specialists
- Parents and students

You will also need to develop a schedule to conduct school site visits.

Discussion Questions

1. What are students in the district expected to know and be able to do?
2. How have these expectations affected graduation requirements?
3. What are the advantages and disadvantages of a closely followed written curriculum?
4. Should all students be held to the same standards regardless of their ability, previous experience, socioeconomic level, and future plans? Why or why not?
5. How can a district ensure quality teaching for all students regardless of the teacher's level of experience?

The Connectivity
and Equity Standard

Standard 3: The school system demonstrates internal connectivity and rational equity in its program development and implementation.

"The left hand doesn't know what the right hand is doing."

"That's not fair!"

"Don't they ever do it the same way twice?"

These are all-too-common laments in many walks of life, but they are particularly pertinent in school systems. Students, staff, parents, and the community share fundamental beliefs about quality in education—they expect school districts to be consistent, fair, and predictable. They want to know that their children can get the best possible education regardless of grade, subject, or site. They want to have a role in determining what most needs to be done. They want to know how to help get things done.

Audit Standard 3 addresses the needs for all aspects of the school district to be appropriately linked to one another. This linkage ensures that all elements of the school experience are connected so that the curriculum can be articulated and coordinated. This linkage also helps guarantee that access to courses, facilities, technology, discretionary funds, quality leadership, and other aspects of the district are in keeping with the needs of the school population. The goal of connectivity and equity is to provide every student and staff person with the monitoring, staff development, teaching quality, resource allocation, and decision-making support to provide for a continuing cycle of improvement.

What the Auditor Expects to Find

The curriculum management auditor looks for answers to four questions in Standard 3:

1. Does the district link all of its operation to the mission?
2. Are these linkages adequately monitored?
3. Do individual elements of the system—namely, staff development, teaching quality, resource allocation, and decision making—support the curriculum implementation?
4. Is there equity in program delivery and district operations?

Board policies, long-range plans, budget documents, school schedules, individual site profiles, and memos are among the specific types of documents that are examined.

Connectivity to the Overall System

Understanding the school district's defining mission is the foundation of auditing connectivity. The mission is usually found in a statement of fewer than 100 words. It may be a narrative or in list form. It may be widely distributed and prominently posted, or it may be relatively inaccessible and go largely unread. If it is used to connect the district's operations, it is likely to be easy to find, easy to memorize, and easy to see in action.

Typical district mission statements focus on three things: student achievement, the environment, and a future focus. A sample mission statement might read as follows:

> We, the staff, students, and community of Pleasant Land School District, unite to increase student achievement, provide a safe and positive learning environment, and prepare students to be productive citizens in the 21st century.

It is generally supported with a board policy that delineates more precisely what "increase student achievement" means. The board policy provides for a budget that balances academic materials with deferred maintenance. It also calls for minutes of meetings that explain how staff and parents are actively involved in the decisions of the school. Finally, it accounts for the equipment and staff needed to provide ongoing training and opportunities to use technology as a routine part of the instructional program.

Linkage

Alignment of the written, tested, and taught curriculum is the key relationship that the auditor examines. The following operational elements should be clearly aligned with the fundamental goals of the curriculum:

- A board-adopted mission statement
- The budget
- Goal statements in all major planning documents, including the strategic plan, school improvement plans, deferred maintenance plans, and others
- Instructional, assessment, and staff development focus statements

The auditor looks for evidence in written documents that these linkages exist. The auditor also probes for a commitment to these linkages through interviews by asking such questions as

What is the adopted mission of this district? What is the real mission? How do you know?
Who determined the mission?
In which documents can the mission statement be found?
If you wanted to spend money for something that is not expressly supported by the mission statement, what barriers would you encounter?
Are all schools and programs equally committed to the mission?
How can parents be sure that their child will get the same quality of instructional program regardless of grade or subject at schools in this district?

The auditor typically characterizes problems with linkages as "uneven," "inadequate," "inconsistent," "limited," "poorly communicated," "incomplete," "worsening," "decreasing," or "compromised." The auditor is looking for evidence that the linkage is supporting consistency to a degree that all staff and students are equally supported in their work, all grades and subjects offer the same level of quality regardless of site, and the linkages prove reliable.

Monitoring Curriculum Implementation

The district may have attractively packaged curriculum filling shelves in a lovely conference room at the central office. However, if that curriculum is not readily available to the teacher who needs it, there is a minimal chance that it is being effectively implemented. Similarly, if the teachers have never seen the documents used to test their students, it is unlikely that there is a clear match between what is taught and what is tested. When this kind of mismatch goes unchecked, teachers frequently retreat to the privacy of their classrooms, withdraw from participation in discussions about how to increase student achievement, and panic if a visitor comes through the door—all because they are not sure they are doing what they are supposed to be doing.

Teachers are stifled in poorly managed systems such as these. They must rest assured that what they are doing is in the best interest of their students and is on the guide adopted by the board. Only then can they be free to do their most effective work.

Monitoring the implementation of the curriculum meets this need. Effective monitoring occurs at several levels:

- *The classroom* in which the teacher develops written lesson plans that reflect the objectives, activities, and resources of the curriculum guide
- *The school building* in which the principal, mentors, and resource teachers regularly observe the teacher and provide feedback
- *The district office* in which curriculum specialists and support staff responsible for research and evaluation, special projects, staff development, instructional materials, technology, and public information provide the school with an analysis that is based on observations, interviews, test scores, demographic data, and other standardized information

The auditor looks for evidence that an effective monitoring system is in place. Most typically, the auditor asks the teacher how often the principal visits in the classroom. The response will indicate if the teacher thinks the amount of time is sufficient to promote quality feedback. The auditor also asks the principal how often he or she visits in the classroom to compare the principal's response with that of the teacher. Frequently these numbers bear little similarity.

The auditor is also interested in information about how often teachers use outside assistance, how accessible their curriculum guide is, how they know what will be tested, and who they talk to about lessons and activities.

Quality systems for monitoring curriculum begin and end with written data. In an effective system, people replace the phrase *I feel that* with *I know.* They can cite accurate statistics with understanding. The auditor—to compare people's answers to interview questions with up-to-date statistics—

must refer to written documents that summarize the student population in terms of

- The total number of students
- The number of students by gender and ethnicity
- Mobility
- Retention
- Dropout rates
- Placement in special programs, such as those for special education, gifted and talented education, and free and reduced meals

These documents should be consistent in format, accurate, complete, readily available, and current.

The auditor typically characterizes problems with monitoring as follows:

There is no system.
The system is on paper but not in practice.
Monitoring is inconsistent or inadequate.
The system does not promote accountability.
The system is unresponsive to district regulations.

The auditor is looking for evidence that monitoring is occurring as an ongoing part of the life of the school.

Staff Development

A district's commitment to staff development can become a community controversy. Every day that teachers are away from school or school is not in session compromises the fundamental service parents expect from schools: caretaking. Parents are inconvenienced and, in some cases, students' safety is jeopardized because the arrangements made for their care are inadequate.

In addition, staff development is expensive. The cost of replacing a teacher for the day, even with a substitute, is likely to exceed $100 in salary and operational costs. The teacher then needs mileage, meals, and fees for the training or conference he or she is attending. Even a "free" workshop can cost several hundred dollars, times the number of teachers who participate, times the number of training sessions conducted. Add administration of reimbursements, and pretty soon you are talking about real money.

The biggest cost of all, however, is the cost of inadequately prepared teachers. Whether they are novices or award-winning veterans, their education and experience must be continually upgraded if they are to apply engaging learning strategies, use new materials, and teach new subjects. It is incumbent upon the district to invest in its employees to ensure that they are prepared for the tasks they are assigned. Only by creating a program of staff development—one that is clearly linked to the instructional focus of the district—can the district hold teachers accountable for the changes they are expected to make.

Auditors typically characterize problems with staff development as "inadequate," "unplanned," "haphazard," "uncoordinated," or "unsupported." They frequently find that there is no system that ties what teachers want to execute with what they are expected to accomplish in the classroom. The auditor is looking for evidence that staff development is clearly linked to the instructional design and the accountability program.

Teaching Quality

In an audit of a large, urban district, after drafting dozens of tentative recommendations, it was suggested that the team submit only one: "Teachers must teach better. Now." Despite a clear mission and a large budget, the quality of teaching observed could only be described as poor.

In the aligned curriculum, written curriculum guides the teaching, teaching guides the testing, and testing guides the revisions to the written curriculum. Neither a written curriculum nor a comprehensive testing program matter if teaching is poor. There are many existing checklists that guide observers in their analysis of teaching quality. The auditor's is quite simple.

The audit looks at three things: what the teacher is doing, what the students are doing, and what resources are available to support them. The teacher is expected to be actively engaged in directing the learning. This may mean that the teacher is the focus of the activity, as in a lecture or demonstration. It could also mean that the teacher is a facilitator, as in a cooperative learning activity, a simulation, an individual or small-group session, or any other activity where the teacher's role is one of guiding.

It does not mean that the teacher is out of the room, chatting with a colleague about the weekend, correcting papers, or conducting side business. The objective of the teacher's instruction should be evident. It should be tied directly to the written curriculum. The evaluation strategy should be evident.

The student is expected to be actively engaged in the learning process. This may mean that the student is working alone or that a group of students is working together. The student may be practicing a new skill, reviewing prior instruction, listening attentively, completing a project, working with technology, or participating in any part of the process of learning.

It does not mean that the student is sleeping, staring into space, passing notes, chatting with peers, doing homework from another class, waiting for instructions, or in any other way squandering the time available to learn. The focus of the student's learning activity should be evident. The student's activities should be clearly tied to that focus. The student should be able to talk about what he or she is learning and why, and the extent to which he or she has learned it.

The auditor looks for teaching that effectively engages students; meets current learning needs while preparing students for the future; is consistent across grades, subjects, and sites; and is tied to the board policies and curriculum guides.

Resource Allocation

Traditionally, education was a fairly inexpensive proposition. Each community banded together to build the school, hire the teacher, and get a small number of books for each student. Field trips were within walking distance, no buses ran, and children brought their lunch. The number of forms submitted to the state was minimal.

Education is fundamentally the same today. However, attach to the mix any number of additions: materials designed to meet the needs and spark the interests of an array of students, widespread use of technology, all-day and overnight field trips, storage facilities, gymnasiums, cafeterias, 90-passenger buses, developer fees, facilities prepared to support the community through numerous disasters, unions, fiscal oversight, and many others. Despite these increases, the district is expected to ensure that all students have access to the resources that they need and that no resources are wasted.

It is simple enough to limit the notion of resources to such tangibles as the number of computers per student or volumes in the library. But the auditor must also examine the equitable distribution of the single resource that generally requires 80 to 90% of the total budget: the staff. The auditor looks for evidence of positions that are misclassified or inappropriately paid. These may be salaried employees who no longer provide any service or those who, in lieu of termination, have been given some low-priority assignment for several years prior to retirement.

The auditor typically identifies problems such as resources that are inconsistently distributed, resources that do not provide equitable educational opportunities, specific practices (such as charging participation fees) that promote inequities, and resources that are not tied directly to program implementation.

Decision Making

Since the advent of site-based decision making, the ability of a school district to remain connected has been seriously challenged. The district office may believe that it is has clearly and thoroughly communicated its learning expectations, only to be asked by a kindergarten teacher what to teach. In some schools, the time taken to write rules of order, resolve disputes, or argue about what consensus really means has left staff asking: "Why won't someone just tell us what to do?" The community is left with concerns about the amount of time it takes to get things done, especially when told that there will be no school Friday because teachers have a meeting with a high-paid speaker who will help them resolve their conflicts.

The goal of site-based decision making is to be certain that the general goals of the organization are implemented in the best possible way at the local level. In education, this means that the board policies direct the school, which in turn creates specific implementation plans. In such a system, schools are free to pilot projects, explore promising practices, and create school-based improvement plans that respond to the needs of the student body.

The auditor looks for evidence that decision making is founded upon the board's policies. Problems include situations in which site-based decision making has demoralized the staff, diminished consistency in curriculum design or delivery, been inconsistently implemented, and not been connected to the overall instructional focus.

Auditing Connectivity

To conduct the audit for connectivity, the auditor completes Exhibit 7.1.1. This form provides a checklist to identify areas in which the district is lacking linkages. The auditor uses documents, interviews, and observations to find evidence of problems in these areas.

Two of the linkage areas require more extensive analysis. The first of these is teaching quality. The auditor uses Exhibit 7.1.2 while observing teachers at work. Copies of this exhibit can be made for each observation; it can also be used by the auditor to summarize the overall observations.

The second linkage for which additional analysis is required is resource allocation. Exhibit 7.1.3 is used to guide questioning about resources.

Equity in the Overall System

Treating students in accordance with the differences in their needs is fundamental to providing educational equity. This does not mean treating them exactly the same, because they are not all the same to begin with. It means providing the resources needed to support each student as he or she works to attain the highest goals of the district.

A district with educational equity is interested in students as individuals—not as groups, not by grades, not in classes. The staff meeting conversation is peppered with comments about individual student differences and how each student is doing. Teachers know the varying strengths and weaknesses of students and provide instruction related to that understanding.

At the site level, equity means providing the different resources needed by individual students. The success of this strategy has been most evident in two parts of the overall system: in special education, where student disabilities have been diagnosed and resources for those disabilities provided; and

(text continues on page 75)

Standard 3—Exhibit 7.1.1

Connectivity Assessment

Each question below was audited. The auditor used written documents, observations, and interviews to determine the answer. For each question, at least two of these sources were used to find the answer.

Question	Evidence Sources
Mission Linkages 1. Does the staff know the adopted mission of the district?	

2. Is the mission supported by
   a. the board?
   b. Budget?
   c. Planning activities?
   d. Staff?	

3. Is there any mission besides the adopted one?	
Monitoring Curriculum Implementation 4. How is curriculum monitored in the classroom?	
5. How is curriculum monitored in the building?	
6. How is curriculum monitored in the district?	
7. What are the biggest problems with curriculum monitoring?	
Staff Development 8. How does the staff development program support the mission and instructional program?	
9. What formats are used for staff development?	
10. What topics have been covered in staff development?	
Teaching Quality 11. What are the teaching strengths in the district?	
12. What are the teaching weaknesses in the district?	
Resource Allocation 13. How are resources allocations determined?	
14. What are the biggest resources issues facing the district?	

Adapted from audits sponsored by American Association of School Administrators' National Curriculum Audit Center.

Standard 3—Exhibit 7.1.2

Teaching Quality Checklist

The auditor assessed teaching in _____ classroom observations. Particular attention was paid to the characteristics listed below. A check in the right column indicates that teaching was not of optimal quality.

Characteristic	*Concern*
1. The teacher is in classroom.	
2. Teaching time is well used.	
3. Teaching materials are appropriately challenging.	
4. Teaching strategies are appropriately engaging.	
5. There is evidence that a variety of strategies are used.	
6. Students are engaged in teacher-directed activities.	
7. Student activities are related to learning objectives.	
8. Student assessment is related to learning objectives.	
9. The teacher seems used to visitations.	
10. There is evidence that work at high standards is expected by teachers and students.	
Other:	

Standard 3—Exhibit 7.1.3

Resource Allocation Checklist

The auditor assessed resource allocation in _____ classroom observations. Particular attention was paid to the characteristics listed below. A check in the right column indicates that resource allocation was not of optimal quality.

Characteristic	Concern

1. The allocation of the following is appropriately related to the instructional program:
 	
  a. Support staff (health, library, clerical, administrative)
 	
  b. Supplemental materials in the classroom
 	
  c. Other supplemental materials (career center, library)
 	
  d. Computers and other technology
 	
  e. Field trips
 	
  f. Classrooms
 	
  g. Play areas
 	
  h. Support facilities
 	
2. Maximum value is made of
 	
  a. Instructional time by teachers and students
 	
  b. Professional development time by teachers and administrators
 	
3. Resources are procured in an efficient manner.
 	
4. Resources are appropriately secured.
 	
5. Resources are appropriate maintained.
 	
Other:	

in alternative education, where personal needs drive the instructional program. In traditional education, equity challenges administrators to provide access to the highest levels of course content to all students. It requires that the best teachers are as likely to teach disadvantaged students as those who are academically gifted. It also means that there is a clear commitment to doing what is right even when it challenges long-standing tradition.

At the district level, it means monitoring the implementation of programs carefully. There must be clear evidence that the decisions made at the school site consistently support the district mission, adhere to the stated values, and follow the policies adopted by the board.

The curriculum management audit is founded upon the belief that all students deserve a quality education every day, regardless of age, gender, ethnicity, grade, socioeconomic level, subject, parental involvement, or site. The auditor typically characterizes problems with equity as "impeding the quality of learning," "inadequate access to specific resources," "commitment that is contradictory or ambiguous," or "increasing."

School funds are most frequently provided in two sums. The first of these is the discretionary budget, which is allocated for expenses other than salaries—such as materials, equipment, capital outlay, repair, contracted services, consultants, deferred maintenance, and other items deemed necessary for the school operation. Typically the amount is set per pupil, with some district funds used to meet supplemental needs, such as major building remodeling, roof repair, plumbing replacement, and legal mandates.

The second sum of funds provided to a school is the staff allotment. This is frequently a fixed amount per pupil across schools and usually represents 80% to 90% of the total budget. In most districts, schools are given a certain number of teachers, counselors, administrators, clerical staff, custodians, and librarians in accordance with the overall student enrollment. These are kept proportionate throughout the district. In some districts, each school is given the latitude to trade or convert certificated, classified, and management staffing units. School X may use the allotment to provide 2 primary grade teachers, whereas School Y uses the allotment for 1 primary grade teacher and 2 instructional support staff. This flexibility may lead to the appearance of equity issues if some schools provide services that are not available at other schools. It is the auditor's task to determine if the differentiation meets the needs of the students served.

Auditing Equity

Money is the key to equity. The auditor should be able to chart the budget development process, including its relationship to the state budget process, the site's needs, the district's policies, and the roles played by staff and community. This accounting should include general fund monies and all special funds, such as food services, deferred maintenance, building, transportation, special reserves, and stores.

The auditor then examines the amount of money the district provides to the school or program through the basic allotment and through special allotments. Exhibit 7.2.1 is used to identify any key differences in the per-pupil allocation of money. Difference does not mean that there is an equity issue; however, it prompts the auditor to find out why the difference exists. If the allocation enables the school to treat students in accordance with the differences in their needs, it will not constitute a finding. If, however, the allocation provides disproportionate funding based on ethnicity, for example, it will result in a finding of inequity.

Exhibit 7.2.2 examines the schools' second sum of support: staff allocation. Documents such as policies on personnel allocation, staffing ratio guidelines, affirmative action reports, and site requests form the basis for understanding how staff allocation decisions are made. Interviews and observations are used to arrive at conclusions about the equity of staffing allocations.

Once the full-time equivalent allocation is known, the auditor looks at how the allocation is actually used to provide courses. Exhibit 7.2.3 produces a list of all courses and the number of sections offered at the districts' sites. This process is greatly simplified if the district uses a common code and title for each course. If not, the auditor has to make some judgments about course equivalents, which may lead to a recommendation for uniformity. In using the form, the auditor lists all courses offered within one subject area, such as language arts or social studies. If a common code is available, it is listed. Then the name or site code of each school is listed and new columns are drawn on the right. The number of sections of each course is added and totaled at the bottom. This enables the auditor to see obvious differences in the variety of courses and the number of basic, remediation, and enrichment options at each site.

Justifying Differences

The auditor can use many characteristics to justify different resource allocations. Most of these, however, create unjustifiable differences of their own. The curriculum management audit process analyzes differences on the basis of student achievement, usually measured by standardized test scores. Although not a perfect measure, the district that is paying serious attention to an assessment program will have focused on test performance. This focus drives accountability and program improvement—both of which, inevitably, lead to requests for resources to be used in new and better ways.

Exhibit 7.2.4 provides for a comparison between test scores and money (whether it is personnel or nonpersonnel funding). In this exhibit, schools are listed in rank order from high achieving to low achieving. In the next column, their ranks are entered in order of per-pupil allotment. The auditor examines this data to identify patterns and equity issues.

(text continues on page 81)

Standard 3—Exhibit 7.2.1

Basic and Supplemental Allotment Formulas

The first column contains the name of the school or program. The second column is the amount, per pupil, of the basic allotment for all student expenses. The third column is the amount, per pupil, of additional funds for all student expenses. The two allotments are totaled and listed in the fourth column.

Name	Basic	Supplemental	Total

Standard 3—Exhibit 7.2.2

Staffing Allotment Formulas

The first column contains the name of the school or program. The second column is the full-time equivalent, per pupil, of the administrative staff. The third column is the full-time equivalent, per pupil, of certificated staff. The fourth column is the full-time equivalent, per pupil, of classified staff.

Name	Administrative	Certificated	Classified

Standard 3—Exhibit 7.2.3

Course Allotment Formulas

Subject _____

Page _____ of _____

The column on the left is the course title. The common course code, if there is one, is in the middle column. The right column represents the number of sections of the course at each school audited.

Course Title	Code	School Names and Number of Sections
Total		

Standard 3—Exhibit 7.2.4

School Achievement and Allotment Rankings

The first column contains the name of the school or program, listed in order of ranking on the district's achievement test. The second column is the achievement rank from highest to lowest. The third column is the rank on per-pupil allocation from Exhibit 7.2.1. The fourth column is the dollar amount allocated per pupil.

School or Program	Achievement Rank	Allocation Rank	Amount

Other Connectivity and Equity Issues

Every district will have issues that are unique to its history and operation. The following exhibits provide the auditor with tools to present information about those areas that are of concern.

Exhibit 7.3.1 analyzes the support given to any individual budget item. This may be used for such expenses as computer equipment, field trips, supplemental materials, staff development, or other resources that are an issue in the district. The auditor identifies the expense category being allocated, one per page, enters the names of the schools or programs, lists the school's total enrollment, the total budget for the item being analyzed, and the per-pupil value (the total divided by the enrollment).

Exhibit 7.3.2 analyzes the ratio of minority students and teachers for a 2-year period. This exhibit may be used to demonstrate the difference in this ratio and is of particular interest if the district has affirmative-action policies.

Exhibit 7.3.3 analyzes the percentage of special-population students in schools. The auditor may select the most appropriate populations such as minorities, at-risk students, special-education students, limited-English-proficient students, free- and reduced-lunch recipients, or other special program participants.

Exhibit 7.3.4 analyzes student status by school to provide data about retention, dropout rate, suspensions, or expulsions. This exhibit may be modified: for example, it could include the percentage of minority students rather than the total percentage of students. It may be repeated to track this data over 2 or more years.

About the Findings

School schedules, handbooks, staff development documents, program budgets, decision-making charts and policies, site visits, and interviews provide the focus for the audit of Standard 3. When this audit has been completed, the district will be able to improve the practices needed to increase connectivity and equity. A review of the curriculum management audits completed in the last 2 years have a number of findings in common that are directly supported by the process provided in this chapter. Typical findings have included the following:

3.1 Connectivity of the Overall System

The linkage of the written, taught, and tested curriculum is uneven (or inadequate, inconsistent, limited, or poorly communicated).

(text continues on page 86)

Standard 3—Exhibit 7.3.1

Budget Item Equity Analysis

For _____

Page _____ **of** _____

The first column contains the name of the school or program. The second column is the total enrollment of the school. The third column is the total amount of money allocated to this item. The fourth column is the amount per pupil for this item (the total divided by the enrollment).

School or Program	Enrollment	Total Value	Amount Per Pupil

Standard 3—Exhibit 7.3.2

Minority Students and Teachers as a Percentage—A 2-Year Analysis

The first column contains the name of the school or program. The second column is the current-year enrollment. The remaining four columns are the percentage of minority students and teaching staff members in the most recently completed school year and the current school year.

School or Program	Current-Year Enrollment	Minorities as a Percentage of Total			
		Students		Teaching Staff	
		Past Year	Current Year	Past Year	Current Year

Kimberly Logan, *Getting the Schools You Want.* Copyright © 1997 by Corwin Press, Inc.

Standard 3—Exhibit 7.3.3

Special Population Enrollment by Program

The first column contains the name of the school or program. The second column is the current-year enrollment. The remaining columns are the percentage of special-population students enrolled in the current school year. Fill in the blanks with the names of each of three special populations analyzed.

School or Program	Current-Year Enrollment	Special Population Percentage Enrollment		
		_____	_____	_____

Standard 3—Exhibit 7.3.4

Student Status as a Percentage of Total Enrollment—
Retentions, Dropout Rates, Suspensions, and Expulsions

The first column contains the name of the school or program. The second column is the current-year enrollment. The remaining columns are the percentage of students who were retained, dropped out, suspended, or expelled in the most recently completed school year.

School or Program	Current-Year Enrollment	Percentage of Students			
		Retained	Dropped Out	Suspended	Expelled

Linkage among parts of the system (e.g., grades, subjects, schools) is limited.

Linkage is impairing internal consistency.

Linkage is ignoring the organizational focus.

Articulation and coordination of the curriculum are limited.

Curriculum consistency is a result of local/state/regional/federal mandates.

The lack of connectivity has been made worse by recent unification/ site-based decision-making/district reorganization.

3.2 Monitoring

There is no system to monitor curriculum implementation at the district (or site) level.

Monitoring curriculum implementation is inconsistent and inadequate.

Curriculum monitoring is lacking specific measures of accountability (or failing to produce effective lessons, or compromised by poor communication with supervisors, etc.).

Data about student dropouts (or free- and reduced-lunch participants, or special-education placements, etc.) is inconsistent (or inaccurate, incomplete, or unavailable).

Curriculum monitoring is unresponsive to board policies and administrative regulations.

3.3 Staff Development

Professional development is supported but is not designed or coordinated systemwide.

Staff development programs/hiring practices are not tied directly to program implementation.

Staff training lacks accountability, planning, focus, or consistency.

3.4 Teaching Quality

Teaching practices are inconsistent, ineffective, or outdated.

The quality of instructional practices varies greatly among grades/ subjects/sites.

Teaching is unresponsive to board policies.

3.5 Resource Allocation

Distribution of financial resources is inconsistent with the need to provide equitable educational opportunities.

The practice of charging fees, transporting students, or providing supplemental materials promotes inequities.

The allocation of materials (or supplies, equipment, or technology) is not tied directly to program implementation.

3.6 Decision Making

Innovations/pilot projects/site-based management decisions have diminished consistency in curriculum design and delivery.

Practices to support school-based decision making are inconsistent.

School-based improvement plans are not connected to the overall district instructional focus.

3.7 Equity

Inequities impede the quality of student learning, including availability of and access to course offerings (or facilities, technology, discretionary funds, or leadership).

Equity in program delivery and district operations is inadequate and ineffective.

Evidence about the district's commitment to equity is contradictory, ambiguous, unclear, or inadequate to guide effective educational interventions.

Some inequities require central office intervention to resolve.

3.8 Other Connectivity and Equity Issues Unique to the District

The alternative school referrals are ineffective for deterring students from dropping out.

The district has improved connectivity by allocating differentiated resources (or implementing a new communications technology, or adopting board policies).

Communication from the central office to the school sites is inconsistent, inadequate, incomplete, late, or inaccurate.

Articulation with feeder districts is inadequate.

Concerns exist regarding treatment of students and staff.

The district does not adequately hire and replace administrative (or teaching or support staff) positions.

Preparing to Audit Standard 3

To audit this standard, you will need to gather the following documents:

- Board policies
- Long-range plans and activity calendars for staff development, deferred maintenance, technology, and others

- Budget documents showing all general and special-fund income and expenditures
- School schedules with course titles and bell schedule
- Individual site profiles or school report cards with demographic and assessment information
- Memos on topics related to connectivity and equity
- The district's mission statement
- Grant applications
- Instructional, assessment, and staff development focus statements
- Curriculum guides
- Decision-making and communication flowcharts

Make arrangements to interview the following:

- Key central office staff responsible for budgets, special projects, support services, human resources, and affirmative action
- Key site staff responsible for instruction including the principal, curriculum director, resource teachers, and both new and veteran teachers
- Parents and students

You will also need to schedule observations of all facilities and classrooms.

Discussion Questions

1. What examples from your own workplace provide concerns about connectivity? About equity?
2. How would improvements in connectivity improve the perception the community has of schools?
3. To what degree is it reasonable to hold schools to an equity standard?
4. What are the biggest impediments to connectivity and equity?
5. What decision-making "rules" would help to ensure a high quality standard of education for all students in a district?

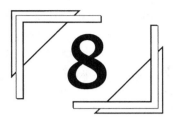

The Assessment Standard

Standard 4: The school system uses the results from system-designed or -adopted assessment to adjust, improve, or terminate ineffective practices or programs.

Many newspaper columns, speeches, and conversations begin with the notion that public education has failed. This assumption has become so pervasive that few people seem to even blink when they hear it. Of course, they love their child's teacher, and they generally like their local school. It is those other schools in other areas where this presumed failure has occurred.

There seem to be several lessons here. Although they can be reduced to poster-sized sentiments, they are nevertheless true.

The first is that people do not like what they do not know. It is comparatively easy to take random shots at other people's schools if you do not know the people involved or what they do.

The second is that schools are regarded as democracy's saving grace. To the extent that a citizenry is concerned about the stability of its governmental institution, so it shall be concerned about the quality of its educational institution. If the government is troubled by financial, social, or world events, it seems there must be something wrong with how students are being prepared.

The third is that everyone is an expert about schools. Everyone has attended a school. Everyone has had experiences upon which to base their judgment. Everyone has had one or more really bad experiences, academic or personal, while in school. Therefore, schools must be failing today since bad things happened to us when we were there 20 or 30 or 40 years ago.

Some schools are failing some students. Some schools may be failing a lot of students. But America's schools are providing higher levels of achievement for more students than ever before. They have simply forgotten to tell the staff and community.

Nearly all students are subjected to some kind of assessment every day. The teacher may observe that half of the students have caught on to the skill. The teacher may collect papers that show which students have mastered the content. The student may perform the skill or complete the standardized test or return the checklist of tasks accomplished or submit any number of assessments that are a routine part of school life.

Some of these assessments will end up as student grades, on an individual paper or a report card. Some will go to the district office where analytical multicolor, multidimensional graphs will be constructed. Some will make their way into annual reports and newspaper headlines. Many will have been of transitory use to the student or the teacher. Most may have served little, if any, purpose at all.

The school district that is committed to improvement will have a system for using feedback through agreed-upon assessment strategies. This system will include provisions for how and when data will be collected. It will include multiple measurements of the key areas of concern. Most important, it will use the assessment data to adjust, improve, and terminate ineffective practices and programs.

What the Auditor Expects to Find

The curriculum management auditor looks for answers to six questions in Standard 4:

1. What does the district test?
2. What tests are used in the assessment program?
3. How long have the tests been used?
4. What information do the tests provide?
5. Who uses the data?
6. What decisions are made with the data?

The first four questions focus on the design of the assessment program. The last two define the program's delivery. They combine to determine if the curriculum meets the standards set by the district, if student achievement meets district expectations, and if the instructional program is effective in meeting the objectives defined in the curriculum. An audit of the assessment system focuses on what students are to learn (the curriculum) and the manner in which the objectives are met (the instruction). Fundamental to the Standard 4 audit is the understanding that test data should provide feedback upon which instruction can be improved.

Assessment Scope

Written curriculum guides should be available for every subject that is taught in the district. As part of these guides, an assessment plan should be evident. The assessment design must provide data that can be used to help the staff do four tasks:

1. Analyze trends in the instructional program
2. Modify or terminate programs that are ineffective
3. Identify emerging curriculum needs
4. Guide decisions about curriculum and instruction

An adequate assessment design provides staff with data that support both short- and long-term planning. The key documents used to audit the scope and design of the assessment program are curriculum guides and program evaluation documents. Three forms are used to determine the scope and adequacy. The first, Exhibit 8.1.1, requires that the auditor list each formal test given in the previous year in the column on the left. In the columns for each grade, one of three marks is entered to designate the nature of the test administration.

B = Benchmark test—passage is required for graduation or satisfactory course completion
R = Required test for all students
O = Optional test taken by some students

Once this matrix is completed, the auditor has information about the scope of the most recent assessment design. It is also important to identify changes this represents by determining how long these tests have been used. Exhibit 8.1.2 is used to record this information. In the left column, the auditor enters the name of each test given in any of the previous 5 years. An "X" is entered to show each year the test was given.

Exhibit 8.1.3, a matrix of formal texts administered by discipline, is used to audit the scope and design of the assessment program. This is a variation of Exhibit 8.1.1, which listed tests by grade. This matrix determines which subject areas are being tested. The courses that were identified in Exhibit 8.1.1 are listed in the left column. The names of the tests entered on Exhibit

(text continues on page 95)

Standard 4—Exhibit 8.1.1

Matrix of Student Tests Currently Administered

School Year _____

Test	Grade												
	K	1	2	3	4	5	6	7	8	9	10	11	12

Key: B = Benchmark   R = Required   O = Optional

Adapted from audits sponsored by American Association of School Administrators' National Curriculum Audit Center and Frase et al. (1995, p. 193).

Standard 4—Exhibit 8.1.2

Matrix of Student Tests Administered Historically

School Years_____ to _____

Test	Previous^{+3}	Previous^{+2}	Previous^{+1}	Previous	Current

Key: B = Benchmark   R = Required   O = Optional

Adapted from audits sponsored by American Association of School Administrators' National Curriculum Audit Center.

Standard 4—Exhibit 8.1.3

Matrix of Student Tests Administered by Subject

School Year _____

Subject	*Grade*												
	K	*1*	*2*	*3*	*4*	*5*	*6*	*7*	*8*	*9*	*10*	*11*	*12*
Language Arts/English													
Math													
Social Studies													
Science													
Fine Arts													
Physical Education/Health													
Career Education													
Technology Education													
Electives/Other:													

Key:

Test Name	Code	Test Name	Code

Adapted from audits sponsored by American Association of School Administrators' National Curriculum Audit Center and Frase et al. (1995, p. 194).

8.1.1 are listed at the bottom and given a 1- to 3-digit code. This code is entered for each grade level in which the test is given.

These forms enable the auditor to find answers to the first three questions (what does the district test, what tests are used in the assessment program, and how long have the tests been used?). As a result, the auditor can provide information to the district about the scope and design of its assessment program. Understanding the adequacy of the assessment program is critical to improving it. The next step, finding out what information the tests provide, is critical to improving instruction.

Data Analysis

In this section, the auditor provides information about the test results. First, the auditor looks at what the scores are. Are they high or low? Are they consistent across grades, buildings, and classes? Are there any anomalies or unusual scores? This will enable the auditor to determine the degree to which the student scores show acceptable levels of achievement.

Then the auditor looks at data over time: What trends do the data show? Are scores up? Are they down? Are they the same? Is there a pattern?

Finally, the auditor may choose to look at the data as it compares to other groups. Typically, norm-referenced tests enable the analyst to determine if the scores are higher or lower than the national average. Some test administrators provide mean scores for the local and regional administration as well as the national scores. They may provide them by sex or ethnic group. The auditor looks for how well the local students are doing in comparison to these groups.

Exhibit 8.2.1 is used to record trend data for tests by subject. Because of the variation in testing data available among districts, this exhibit is adaptable for use according to subject, grade, and year. The auditor can select the best ways to present the information. Examples are provided in Exhibits 8.2.2, 8.2.3, and 8.2.4.

Data Use

The district may have a comprehension assessment program in which testing occurs at every grade in every subject. It may have reams of reports analyzing the data and the trends. But if no one uses the data, neither the design nor the data are of any value. The ways in which the data are used is the third critical component of this standard.

Three activities define quality use of data:

(text continues on page 100)

Standard 4—Exhibit 8.2.1

Student Test Results

Subject   _____

Grade   _____

Year(s)   _____

Comparison   _____

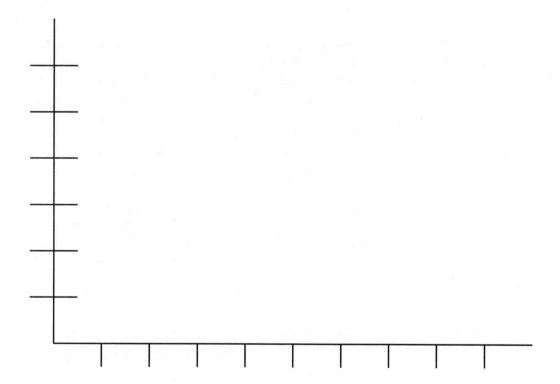

Analysis

Adapted from audits sponsored by American Association of School Administrators' National Curriculum Audit Center.

Standard 4—Exhibit 8.2.2

Sample 1—Student Test Results

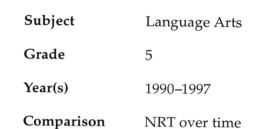

Subject	Language Arts
Grade	5
Year(s)	1990–1997
Comparison	NRT over time

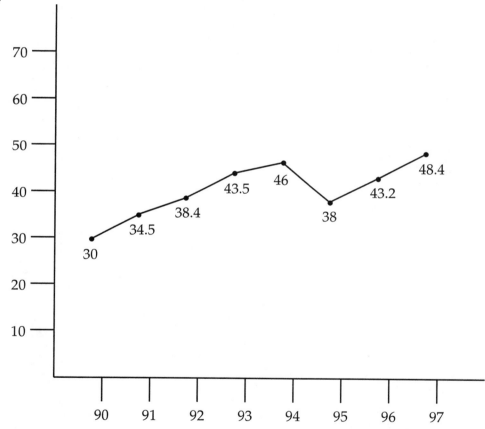

Analysis of Language Arts, Fifth Grade

Normed curve equivalent has ranged from the 1990 low of 30 to the 1997 high of 48.4. Except for one decrease in 1995, scores have increased annually. If this trend continues, the scores can be expected to reach or exceed 50 by 1999.

Standard 4—Exhibit 8.2.3

Sample 2—Student Test Results

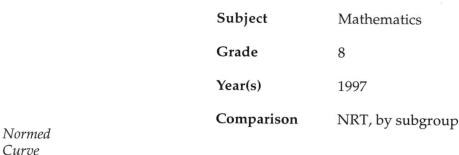

Subject	Mathematics
Grade	8
Year(s)	1997
Comparison	NRT, by subgroup

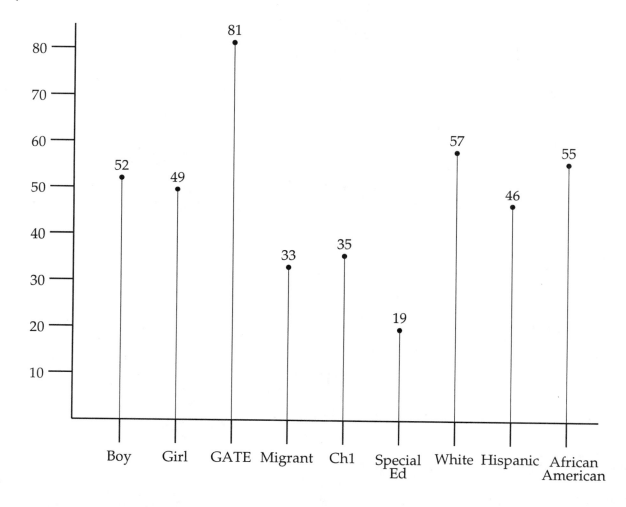

Analysis of Mathematics, Eighth Grade

Boys did better than girls. GATE students did significantly better than other special populations. Whites and African Americans received comparable scores significantly above Hispanic students, whose scores are likely to have been affected by low achievement of migrant students.

Standard 4—Exhibit 8.2.4

Sample 3—Student Test Results

Subject	Spelling
Grade	4
Year(s)	1997
Comparison	Criterion test, by school

Percentage at or
above grade level

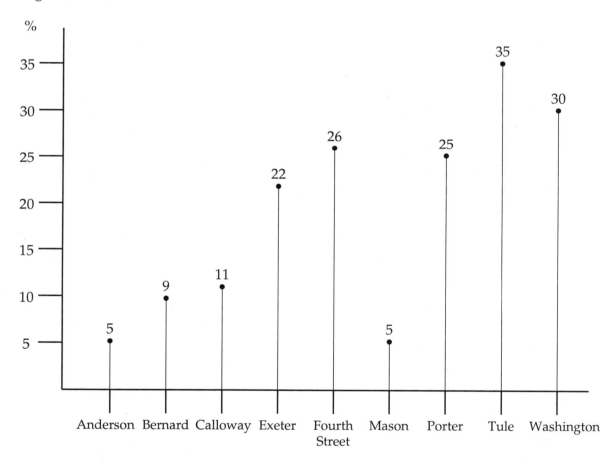

Analysis of Spelling, Fourth Grade

Scores range across schools from a low of 5% above grade level at Anderson and Mason to highs of 35% above grade level at Tule and 30% above grade level at Washington. There is a significant difference among schools.

1. Disaggregation of the data
2. Use of data to create understanding of the status of the written and taught curriculum
3. Use of data to control the quality of the curriculum

Disaggregation

After the drudgery of annual standardized testing, teachers generally receive a report of results. On the form is the name and identification information for each student tested. Then, for each test administered, there is a series of numbers: 2.5, 12-6, 729, and so on. Somehow these numbers are translated into the answer to one question: Did my students learn?

Because of the limits of time and use of the information, teachers and administrators have typically been content to provide such answers as

A lot of kids learned a lot last year.
I could have you told that Johnny was low. Just look at these scores.
How can they expect me to teach that kid anything? He was only here for 4 months.

However, as teachers and administrators become more sophisticated users of the information, the nature of their questions will change. They will begin to ask

Which subtests indicate a clear need for a change in my curriculum?
Did my students make year-for-year growth?
Are there some categories of students who are having more difficulty than others? For example, what differences do limited-English-proficient students show on reading acquisition skills when compared with other students? Are gender and racial stereotypes proving true in my students' math achievement?
What is the profile of those students who have been in the class all year compared with those who entered late?
Do the special education students show any surprising strengths or weaknesses?

When people begin to use data to answer these questions, they will discover the need to "disaggregate" the data. Disaggregation is simply looking at the data by identifiable categories. Usually, these categories include:

- Gender
- Ethnicity
- Mobility
- Special program placement (e.g., special education, gifted and talented, or physically challenged students)

- Language status (e.g., limited-English-proficient and fully-English-proficient students)
- Grade
- School
- Teacher
- Calendar year (e.g., year-round or traditional school schedule)
- Socioeconomic status (frequently coded to free- and reduced-lunch participants)

There are other categories that can be used, such as parents' education level; however, care needs to be taken to ensure that the analysis produces recommendations about how the students' program can be improved. Sending the parent back to school is rarely an option!

Disaggregating data requires planning before implementation of the assessment program. The auditor is interested in which categories are coded and how that decision is made. In many cases, the decision is made in accordance with whatever information is readily available. Less frequently, teachers and administrators determine well in advance of test administration what categories they want. Then they work with the data processors to write a program that will enable them to gather and merge this information.

Exhibit 8.3.1. provides a checklist to determine what categories of information are available in the district's testing programs. These tests are the same ones that were entered in Exhibit 8.1.1.

Evidence of Data Understanding

Districts that use data with understanding will reveal this through evaluation reports and in interviews. The district, especially if it is a midsized or large district, is likely to have a central office department dedicated to providing data analysis. Many schools have a staff member or two whose interest in computer technology has led to an interest in interpreting data. Whether analysis is done centrally or at individual schools, there are likely to be summary reports of test scores, complete with graphs and narrative.

Districts that use data with understanding also have an obvious comfort with discussing, precisely, how their students are doing. They understand basic statistical vocabulary: normed curve equivalents, national and local percentiles, national and local stanines, scale score. They can explain why they do not use grade equivalents and why they do not do fall-to-spring testing as an annual measure of growth. They talk about data with enthusiasm and not as a measure used to identify the "Teacher of the Year." They spend time analyzing raw data and look at multiple measures of a skill before determining that it has been mastered.

Standard 4—Exhibit 8.3.1

Identification of Data Categories Found in Test Reports

Test	Code												
	1	2	3	4	5	6	7	8	9	10	11	12	13

Category Code

1 = Gender
2 = Ethnicity
3 = Mobility
4 = Special program
5 = Language status

6 = Grade
7 = School
8 = Teacher
9 = Calendar year
10 = Socioeconomic status

11 =
12 =
13 =

Adapted from audits sponsored by American Association of School Administrators' National Curriculum Audit Center.

Controlling the Quality of the Curriculum

Once data can be disaggregated and the staff has the skills to understand them, they can be used to improve the instructional program. In most districts, curriculum development is cyclical. Whether the course is a new one being introduced for the first time or is an ongoing course, several phases are usually followed:

Phase 1—Plan new (or review existing) curriculum objectives, scope and sequence, materials and assessment strategies

Phase 2—Revise the written curriculum as needed to support changes in objectives, scope and sequence, materials, assessment

Phase 3—Provide staff training in the implementation of the written curriculum to ensure quality teaching

Phase 4—Monitor progress at predetermined points in the implementation of the written and tested curriculum using appropriate testing measures

Phase 5—Using what was learned in Phase 4, identify changes that are needed

Phase 6—Determine how to incorporate the changes that are needed and return to Phase 1

This cycle is likely to occur over a 5- to 10-year period. Key factors that have an impact on its length include

- The number of new subjects being introduced in the district
- The number of staff members responsible for curriculum development and instruction
- Changes in membership of the governing board
- Information about the subject itself
- Information about how people learn
- Introduction of appropriate new materials and discontinuance of old materials
- Available funds for curriculum development, staff development, and assessment
- Changes in the text adoption or philosophy of the state
- Changes in graduation requirements
- Changes in the student demographic profile

The auditor is interested in all of these factors because they control the pace at which the district can respond to the pressure to change. Quality control can only occur if the district can predict this pace and make a long-term plan addressing the timeline for the six phases.

To determine if Standard 4 is being met, the curriculum management audit focuses on the degree to which assessment has become a high-stakes situation. After the auditor understands the scope and design and has preliminary information about data use, interviews will be conducted to focus on how changes have occurred. Typical audit questions include the following:

> What are you doing differently today compared with several years ago?
>
> What prompted you to make these changes?
>
> What are the most important kinds of data you use to improve your effectiveness?
>
> What other data causes you to change what you do (how you teach, how your monitor teaching)?
>
> What practices that used to be common do you not see much of anymore?
>
> Are there any programs that have been eliminated? What caused their demise?
>
> If your students performed poorly on the key district tests, what would the consequences be (to your students, your program, your school, you)?

The auditor is looking for evidence of the degree to which data are or are not used to make decisions. When data have been used to change practices and programs, there is evidence that this standard is being met.

Other Data

Although test data are critical to making decisions, there are other kinds of data that also are important. These vary by districts and schools. Typical data are those related to

- Enrollment growth
- Changes in the demographic makeup of the student population (especially ethnicity, socioeconomic level, and mobility)
- Attendance rate (real and excused)
- Dropout rate and trend
- Teacher educational level, mobility, and resignation rate

About the Findings

Curriculum guides, evaluation reports, assessment instruments, and interviews provide the focus of Standard 4. When this audit has been completed, the district will be able to develop improvement plans that complete the circle of the written, taught and tested curriculum. A review of curriculum management audits completed in the last 2 years shows that many findings related to scope, analysis of information, and use of information are common to nearly all Standard 4 audits. The sample findings that follow show the range of information the auditor can provide after completing the Standard 4 process.

4.1 Scope

The scope of the assessment program is adequate/inadequate.

The assessment program relies heavily on standardized testing to provide data about most subjects at most grade levels.

The assessment program focus is state driven which results in emphasis on a limited percentage of components of the overall curriculum.

4.2 Data Analysis

Norm-referenced student performances are mixed.

Student assessment data show predictable decline.

Tests show/do not show relatively constant scores over recent years.

Scores on some tests are not improving.

Although test results are generally low, improvement scores are mixed by subject/grade/school.

Evaluation reports are not adequate in form and are limited in scope.

Student test scores are at/below/above the regional/state/national averages.

4.3 Data Use

District generated data are not used in a systematic fashion to make decisions concerning curriculum and instruction.

Assessment is not linked to the curriculum.

Test data are reported widely and do not reflect the entire assessment program.

Test data are inconsistently used by principals and teachers to guide school improvement efforts.

There is no systematic process for use of assessment data in decision making.

The use of student and program assessment is inconsistent.

The data are not used to compare local results with regional/state/national averages.

4.4 Curriculum Management System Structure

There are no goals or expectations against which to mark progress.

Staff development is not clearly tied to instructional needs or school improvement plans.

There is no formal process for the use of student test data as feedback to modify, add, or terminate programs.

Staff feedback indicated the need to _____. (Examples could include prescriptive terms or phrases such as *provide literacy training, discontinue home schooling, increase graduation requirements,* and the like.)

A comprehensive data management plan is nonexistent or inadequate.

Preparing to Audit Standard 4

To audit this standard, you will need to gather the following documents:

- Curriculum guides
- Evaluation reports
- Assessment instruments

Make arrangements to interview the following:

- Research and evaluation staff
- Key site staff including the principal, teachers, mentors, and subject specialists

You will also need to develop a schedule to conduct school site visits.

Discussion Questions

1. What are the pros and cons of "full disclosure" of student assessment results through the media?
2. What barriers block districts from making full use of assessment data?
3. What are some issues related to assessment data likely to be raised by teacher unions?
4. Should a teacher be terminated for poor test results? Under what conditions?
5. Which is the most important component of the aligned curriculum: written, taught, or tested?

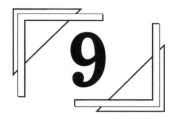

The Productivity Standard

Standard 5: The school system has improved productivity.

A poster in the office hallway declares that if you always do what you have always done, you will always get what you have always gotten. In short, you will not be able to improve your school without changing some of things that are now holding you back. In schools, this means that looking at changes related to facilities, budget development and monitoring, climate, and promising practices is critical to improvement.

What the Auditor Expects to Find

The curriculum management auditor looks for answers to four questions in Standard 5:

1. How well do facilities support the curriculum priorities?
2. What is the relationship between curriculum priorities and how resources are allocated?

3. To what degree does the school and district climate support productivity?
4. What promising practices are in place to support the curriculum priorities?

The primary focus of this standard is on the hurdles and bridges from the board to the school site. Nearly every employee has, at some time, thought that if the board or the district or the government would just go away, he or she could do a better job. This standard examines the ways in which facilities, budgeting, climate, and promising practices have an impact on productivity at the school site.

Facilities

Any good cook knows the importance that facilities play in producing a meal. A kitchen that looks nice somehow produces more pleasing dishes. It is much easier to work in a kitchen with a dishwasher near the sink and a refrigerator close to the food preparation surface. It also works best when the kitchen is organized to minimize accidents and respond to those that do occur. It's nice to have access to all of the appliances, dishware, and tools needed to work. Similarly, a school is more productive if it has facilities that have a pleasant appearance and are suitable, safe, and accessible.

Appearance

The first element of interest to the auditor is appearance. Each district school should have "curbside appeal." As residents drive by and parents drop off children, their impression should be one of a site that is attractive and welcoming. Many schools with growing budget deficits have neglected signage, grounds, and paint. This has not conveyed the message that the school needs help; rather it is has signaled that the school is beyond help. The inside might make Mr. Clean happy but the casual passerby is unlikely to ever come inside and learn this.

The school should also appear orderly and controlled. Some school designs make this easy whereas others make it nearly impossible. Residents and parents will be impressed by a school that shows a place for every student and every student in his or her place. Both playgrounds and classroom areas need to look supervised and well maintained.

Another aspect of appearance is signage. The first words many guests see are "Visitors must report to the office" followed by a list of activities, behaviors, and possessions that are not allowed. Whatever happened to "Welcome to our school—we are happy to have you here"? Beyond the sign that mandates one's visit to the office is a maze of hallways and corridors—but no sign pointing the way there. In a productive school, signs are used to greet; provide essential information; and notify students, staff, and visitors about expectations.

Suitability

Some districts are scrambling to house students in every conceivably appropriate space. Computers labs are tucked into former conference rooms. The stage accommodates sixth graders. Partitions in the cafeteria provide some visual privacy for the intermediate classes while students eat outside or in their classroom. Churches are petitioned for weekly use of their Sunday school classrooms.

In other districts, whole schools are being rented out to private users. Libraries are expanding into two or more classrooms. Teachers and aides have their own office areas. Part of the facility is offered to numerous social services agencies to provide "one-stop" shops.

Regardless of which of these two extremes a district may be facing, it is critical that every location be used for a suitable purpose. The improving district makes a commitment to facilities' use and planning that will ensure that schools are constructed with current and future needs in mind. The general layout of the plan will be conducive to an attractive, orderly appearance, safe operation, and appropriate access. Sufficient storage will be either built in or provided as stand-alone units. The furnishings will be placed to maximize productivity.

Safety

Nothing, it seems, gets the business manager's attention faster than a sentence that begins: "We have a safety issue." This buzzword can be milked to get money when none was available for instructional supplies. It can get staff positions when no funds were available for classroom aides. And it can get action when the adoption of a new textbook was greeted with lethargy.

Clearly, every facility must be safe. It must be free from obvious and hidden hazards. This includes being well lit both when in regular use and during off-hours. It means that the growing number of electrical cords should be secured. Safety-related equipment such as fire alarms, telephone systems, and security systems should be in good working order at all times. Safety notices should be clearly posted in the languages read by users. At a minimum, these notices must indicate the location of fire extinguishers, exits, hazardous materials, telephones, security staff, through traffic, and the first-aid kit. A site safety committee may determine that there are other notices needed at the location.

Access

Since the 1990 passage of the Americans with Disabilities Act (ADA), public consciousness about access has been raised considerably. It is critical that the site has safety-related equipment that is accessible. All of the equipment and all of the notices are of no value if the fire extinguisher cannot be removed from its box by someone who needs it. Academic and personal services provided on campus need to be available to everyone for whom they are intended. The needs for student privacy (such as in the restrooms) must be balanced with the need for supervision to ensure safety. Classrooms and offices need to be large enough and the furniture needs to be comfortable enough that they do not compromise the student's ability to be productive.

One of the auditor's frustrations is always that many facility issues cannot be improved upon regardless of the number of recommendations or loudness of the exhortations. But those that can must be. Those that cannot must be recognized so that they will not be repeated.

These four elements—appearance, suitability, safety, and access—form the basis for the auditor's concern about facilities. Exhibit 9.1.1 provides the auditor with a checklist to use while visiting the district's sites. A check in the far right column indicates that there is a problem that needs to be addressed.

Resources

"Shall we buy a riding lawnmower this year?" Probably not when the first-grade teachers need new readers.

One of the greatest challenges facing school districts whose resources seem to be shrinking as their needs are expanding is balancing the needs of the business with the operation of the business itself. Many school districts are among the community's largest employers. They may purchase more local goods and services than anyone else. They pump a large percentage of total revenue into the community through salaries and benefits packages. They invest their reserve in the local bank and they borrow funds for cash flow and facilities. School districts are clearly a business and are expected to be managed like one. In the private sector, this means establishing equipment-replacement schedules, planning maintenance ahead of crisis, investing in staff training, and managing assets.

In schools, the needs are immediate and plentiful. The classroom teacher needs more supplies and equipment, increased access to on-line services, ceilings that do not leak when it rains, and ongoing training. This results in the proverbial battle: lawnmowers versus readers.

To assess the budget, the curriculum management auditor needs to answer three questions.

1. **Is there sufficient evidence that the curriculum relates directly to the budget?** A combination of the board policies, strategic plan, and the

Standard 5—Exhibit 9.1.1

Facilities Productivity

Page _____ of _____

Location Observed _____ **Date** _____ **Time** _____

During the visit to this location, the following elements were audited by observation. A mark in the column at the right indicates that the element question was answered "No" when observed.

Element Question	No
Appearance 1. Is the location attractive and welcoming? 2. Does it appear orderly and controlled? 3. Are signs used to greet, inform, and notify? 4. Other:	
Suitability 5. Is all of the location being used for suitable purposes? 6. Is the general layout conducive to productive use? 7. Does the location have sufficient storage? 8. Is furniture placed to maximize productivity? 9. Other:	
Safety 10. Is the location free from hazards? 11. Is the location well lit? 12. Are electrical cords secured appropriately? 13. Is safety-related equipment in good working order (e.g., fire alarms, telephones, security systems, etc.)? 14. Are appropriate safety notices posted? 15. Other:	
Access 16. Is safety-related equipment accessible? 17. Can all services used by staff and students be accessed by all users? 18. Is privacy limited to areas where it is appropriate (e.g., the restrooms) but avoided where it is inappropriate (e.g., hallways)? 19. Are rooms and offices sufficient in size and furnishing to be comfortable to users? 20. Other:	

Notes:

curriculum will establish the key priorities of this district. These may include the ability to read by third grade, making a successful transition from primary language to English within 3 years, higher-level problem-solving skills, science literacy, technology use, or any number of other worthy goals. They may be supported with staff development, plans for new materials, and facility modifications. Whatever the key priorities are, budget items should be included to support them.

2. Is the amount spent in direct curriculum-related categories deemed appropriate? The actual amount or percentage of the budget allocated to teachers, instructional support staff, materials, supplies, equipment, furniture, and technology is a judgment that represents the district's priorities. A district that says "Teachers are our most valuable resource" and allocates half of the national average for teachers to its own teaching staff is either kidding or badly mistaken.

Likewise, no one will ever be satisfied that all of their needs are met. The district could expend 100% of its annual budget on any one of these categories and still want for more. The auditor needs to ask about the level of satisfaction, identify the disparities, and then decide if the disparities compromise the district's productivity.

3. Is the amount spent in indirect curriculum-related categories deemed appropriate? As with the expenses directly related to curriculum, support services also need to be budgeted. Program management, staff development, communication, and community relations are critical elements in an improving district. Schools, new programs, and special projects need to be administered so that problems can be handled and services can be coordinated with the rest of the district. With the explosion in research about how people learn and with advances in technology, staff training is increasingly critical to the productive employee. Nothing presents a greater nemesis to productivity than the lack, inadequacy, or inaccuracy of communication. No opportunity is more sorely missed than the opportunity to seize the support of the community.

Although the business manager is usually the expert on the allocation of funds, many people play a role in determining how funds will be allocated. The auditor needs to understand what process is used. A curriculum-driven budgeting process will include administrators responsible for curriculum development and assessment, personnel who specialize in staff development, committee representatives with expertise on a particular subject matter working on curriculum, and personnel involved with grant development. It may include opportunities for all staff and the community to provide input—but nearly every budget will rest, ultimately, in the hands of the governing board. It is their expectation that the budget will reflect the curriculum priorities they have established and that the business of the district will be handled in a professional manner.

In addition to understanding the budget development process that the district uses, the auditor also needs to understand the status of the special funds within the district. Most districts have a general fund which accounts for the general revenue limit from state and local sources. In addition, they usually have special funds for such things as adult education, food services, long-term debt, special education, special reserves, state and federal projects, stores, and transportation. The general fund must have a positive ending balance or it is deficit spending. Unchecked, deficit spending is a precursor to bankruptcy. Special funds, on the other hand, may have a negative ending balance with the difference between income and expenses charged to the general fund. Sometimes this difference is repaid; however, many times it is not, and this is known as "encroachment." If the amount of the encroachment is large or is increasing, the funds available to meet the board's curriculum priorities will be compromised. The monies allocated for staff development can easily be consumed by transporting students to and from school. The auditor needs to be aware of any special funds that are encroaching and determine if this may have a negative impact on the district's curricular productivity.

The auditor uses Exhibit 9.2.1 to assess budget productivity issues in five areas. For questions that are answered "No," the specific concern is listed on the form.

School Climate

Unlike the data-driven components of most audit standards, school climate has more to do with how things feel than how they may actually be. Many elements affect the degree to which a school is or is not offering a positive school climate. Key issues include the following:

- How well the staff works together in planning activities and communicating
- Relationships with supervisors
- Communication about issues, activities, and mission
- Perceptions about leadership, how decisions are made, and how valuable they are
- Participation in decision making
- Knowledge that students benefit from the instructional program
- Meeting students' needs
- Understanding how things work, especially the budget and repair issues
- Understanding one's own role

Standard 5—Exhibit 9.2.1

Budget Productivity

Budget documents and audit reports were reviewed to answer these questions. A mark in the column at the right indicates that the element question was answered "No."

Element Question	No
1. Is there sufficient evidence that the curriculum relates directly to the budget? Concern:	
2. Is the amount spent in the following categories deemed appropriate? A. Teachers B. Instructional support staff C. Materials/supplies/equipment/furniture D. Technology Concern:	
3. Is the amount spent on the following deemed appropriate? A. Program management B. Staff development C. Communication D. Community relations Concern:	
4. Does the process for budget development include the following? A. Administrators responsible for curriculum development and assessment B. Staff development personnel C. Standing committees for curriculum and subject areas D. Grant development personnel Concern:	
5. Are all programs and funds spending within their income? Concern:	

The auditor can find evidence of these issues in interviews. However, a district that is seriously interested in measuring school climate will do so systematically through the administration of climate assessment surveys. These surveys will be reviewed and used by the staff to set priorities and develop improvement plans.

To audit school climate, the auditor examines surveys, if they are available. If not, interviews based on Exhibit 9.3.1 are conducted with a cross section of employees at selected sites. The auditor looks for evidence which may come in the form of direct answers or in examples of what is seen and heard. Consistent "No" answers become the basis of findings about specific school climate problems.

Promising Practices

Promising practices, also known as interventions, are programs and strategies that are implemented to solve specific problems. They are frequently associated with specially funded projects that use grant funds or a site's discretionary money. Some promising practices begin on a very small scale or as a pilot with the expectation that they will grow and become institutionalized. Others start out large with a commitment to improving as they go along. Promising practices have enabled schools to meet the needs of large groups of students. They have also enabled teachers to get the materials and apply strategies that assist individual students with unique problems.

Some promising practices are directly tied to the mission to increase student achievement or prepare students for the 21st century. Others are designed to meet the emotional and physical needs of difficult or disabled students. Some districts support proposals for interventions with an aura of expectations and clear protocols about how to get funding and approval. Others establish an atmosphere in which risk taking becomes almost a subversive activity.

Regardless of the environment, most districts have dozens of promising practices. These interventions typically use a significant portion of the district's discretionary funds. Because they represent much of the district's creativity, they are an important factor in helping the auditor gather information about a district's productivity. Using Exhibit 9.4.1, the auditor identifies the names of as many promising practices as possible. These may be found in curriculum guides, media releases, and other documents. They may be observed during on-site visits. They may be elicited in interviews with staff. Once the list is completed and the contact person is identified by title, the auditor needs to determine when the practice was first established, when it was evaluated, and the annual cost.

The auditor's focus is on how well the district used funds allocated to promising practices. If there has not been any evaluation, the auditor can

(text continues on page 119)

Standard 5—Exhibit 9.3.1

Climate Survey for _____

Page _____ of _____

Climate assessment documents for this site were reviewed to answer the following questions. A mark in the column at the right indicates that the element question was answered "No." Concerns about the element are listed.

Element Question—Is there evidence that	No
1. The school staff works well together to plan instructional activities? Concern:	
2. Every employee can express his or her opinions without fear of reprisal? Concern:	
3. Every employee has a productive relationship with his or her supervisor? Concern:	
4. Every employee is kept informed about issues and activities related to his or her duties? Concern:	
5. Every employee knows the school's mission? Concern:	
6. Every employee knows his or her role in fulfilling the mission? Concern:	

Element Question—Is there evidence that	*No*
7. The superintendent provides leadership that increases student achievement? Concern:	
8. District administrators use data to make decisions? Concern:	
9. Instructional staff feels valued? Concern:	
10. Teachers are involved in the decisions that affect them? Concern:	
11. Staff members know if students are making sufficient academic progress? Concern:	
12. Students' needs are being met in a timely manner? Concern:	
13. Staff members understand the budget and budget development process? Concern:	
14. Staff members know how to get things and get things fixed? Concern:	
15. Every employee knows he or she is part of a system that is continually improving? Concern:	

Standard 5—Exhibit 9.4.1

Promising Practices Review

Page _____ of _____

Column 1 is for the titles of promising practices currently in place in the district. Column 2 is for the title of the contact person for the practice. Column 3 is for the date the practice was established. Column 4 is for the date the practice was evaluated. Column 5 is the annual cost of the practice.

ID#	Title Of Promising Practice	Contact Person by Title	Date Established	Date Evaluated	Annual Cost
1					
2					
3					
4					
5					
6					
7					
8					
9					
10					
11					
12					
13					
14					
15					
16					
17					
18					
19					
20					

help the district understand that it does not know if it is benefiting from the intervention. If the evaluation has been done but shows serious deficiencies in implementation that remain unaddressed, the auditor may be able to show that the cost of the practice outweighs the benefit. Either way, the district that does not know if its promising practices are worthy of continuous expansion or duplication is not maximizing the value of its effort to meet a need.

About the Findings

Deferred maintenance and building plans, budget documents, climate assessment surveys, evaluations of promising practices, site visits, and interviews provide the focus for the audit of Standard 5. When this audit has been completed, the district will be able to improve the practices needed to increase its productivity. A review of curriculum management audits completed in the last 2 years have a number of findings in common that are directly supported by the process provided in this chapter. Typical findings have included the following.

5.1   Facilities

Facilities are in need of repair.

Some facilities are not adequate for their current use.

Facilities do not universally support emerging instructional needs.

The district's master plan for facilities is neither complete nor systematically updated.

Facilities are inadequate to accommodate district enrollment.

Cleanliness and maintenance of district facilities are inadequate and inconsistent.

Effective instruction is inhibited by inadequate facilities.

The increasing need for facilities is placing unmanageable demands on district resources.

Building maintenance management depletes resources available for the instructional program.

Renovations of facilities are unevenly provided.

5.2   Budgets

Budget planning is not driven by data, district goals, or systemwide priorities.

Budgeting is traditional with inadequate linkage to the curriculum.

Budget information is not sufficiently detailed to provide productive cost analysis.

Emphasis on cost is inadequate to promote systemwide productivity.

Many staff members do not believe that equipment, supplies, services, and instructional materials are provided equitably.

5.3 *School Climate*

School climate is inadequately measured.

School climate is negatively affected by poor communication, unresolved contractual issues, inadequate participation in decision making, inability to access management, or lack of recognition.

5.4 *Promising Practices*

Interventions are inadequately evaluated to ensure productivity.

Interventions to improve educational productivity are partially implemented.

Planned interventions have or have not improved productivity or achieved encouraging results in several programs.

New programs frequently lack commitment from all staff.

There is little evidence of changes made to district services and programs as a result of reports/plans.

Systemwide coordination and monitoring of program interventions is inconsistent and ineffective.

Planning for systemwide interventions to increase student productivity is not adequate.

5.5 *Other Productivity Issues Unique to the District*

Board policies are inadequate to guide increased productivity.

Equipment, supplies, services, and instructional materials are inadequately available for the educational program.

Instructional and information technology has not been maximized.

Preparing to Audit Standard 5

To audit this standard, you will need to gather the following documents:

- School site plans
- Current- and prior-year budgets
- Prior-year audit report
- Any current budget-related documents (examples could include a report to the board advisory committee on finance, an annual report, and the like)

- Climate assessment surveys administered to students, staff, parents, community, or graduates
- Information about strategies implemented within the last 5 years that are currently being used to increase student achievement (examples could include recruitment brochures, research studies, newspaper features, memos, agendas, and the like)

Make arrangements to interview the following:

- The business manager
- The facilities manager
- The maintenance and operations managers
- Site principals
- Key instructional leaders involved with implementing new programs and strategies
- The administrator of any fund that is spending more than its income

Discussion Questions

1. What enhances your own productivity?
2. Which message is sent to the community by classrooms that are in disrepair: We need money or We are not spending our current funds well?
3. How can the district create a balance between funds for lawnmowers and funds for children's books?
4. How might school facilities in the 21st century differ from those we see today?

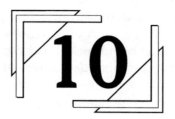

Communicating the
Findings and Recommendations

Parents learn that when they tell their child he or she "has done a dumb thing," the child interprets that as he or she "is dumb." Likewise, auditors learn that telling a district "its organizational chart is inadequate" is perceived as telling the district "*it* is inadequate." Add words like *inconsistent, limited, partially developed, lacking,* and pretty soon you have an overwhelming indictment. It is critical that the auditor presents findings and recommendations in such a way that they can be used to promote positive change.

Findings as Flaws

In the curriculum management audit, findings are expressed as a statement of discrepancy that highlights the difference between what is and what should be:

The evaluation process is nonproductive.
Curriculum guides are inadequate to promote good teaching.

Staff training is not tied to the instructional focus.

There is no formal process to use assessment data as feedback.

Information technology has not been used to maximize productivity.

Each statement details what the situation is. However, the findings that are presented are limited to those that clearly explain what is not being done in keeping with the audit standard. An auditor could easily produce hundreds of findings about curriculum management, but only those that relate to the standards and that provide for curriculum management improvement are presented.

Findings Headings

Each standard has findings that reveal the core of what the audit determined as facts. The finding begins with a heading that states the essence of this fact. Headings are numbered sequentially with the number of the standard first, and key words are capitalized. Headings range in length from about 5 words to 20 and average about 10. They use adjectives to identify shortcomings and tie the facts to the standard.

Findings must pass five tests (English, 1988; see Exhibit 10.1.1). They must be

1. *Unambiguous*—the finding must clearly state what it is meant to state.
2. *Accurate*—the finding must correctly represent the auditor's statement of fact.
3. *Important*—the finding must provide information about the standard that needs to be known; this is also known as the "So what?" test.
4. *Discrepant*—the finding must point to how things should be without stating the auditor's judgment; the finding is not a recommendation.
5. *Specific*—the finding must provide specific information but may use an adjective such as *inadequate* or *ineffective*, which is further defined in the narrative.

Writing quality headings is critical. The heading guides the content of the narrative that follows. Headings are presented in the table of contents, and casual readers will see little more than those headings. If a public presentation of findings is made it will likely be organized by the headings, which will be reported on by the local media. Those who are responsible for making changes will refer to the headings often and will look for recommendations that relate to them.

Exhibit 10.1.1

Activity: Findings Critique

Read each of the findings in the left column below. In the right column, identify any tests that the statement fails.

Finding	Test(s) Failed
Pleasant Land Elementary has 20,000 curriculum guides.	
Student test scores are so poor that the district really should be charged with criminal neglect.	
Three community leaders visited the schools in their European sister city.	
Personnel evaluations cannot be recommended too highly.	
Curriculum improvement is compromised by its one-dimensional, overloaded structural flaws.	
Establish and implement an instructional monitoring process to ensure effective curriculum and instructional practices.	

Hint: If you cannot write the first sentence of the finding with the information you have in the heading, it has failed one or more tests.

The Finding Narrative

After the finding heading comes the narrative. The first paragraph is typically a statement of what the auditor would expect to find in a district that meets the highest standard. This is followed by general statements about what happens when this standard is not met. The auditor uses narratives, bulleted items, and exhibits to present facts that relate to the finding.

Several writing conventions are used in presenting the findings.

- Direct quotes are included to support the finding. They are never directly attributed to the speaker who may be referred to as "a principal," "a special-ed student," "a new teacher," or any member of a larger group. They would not be referred to as a member of a group in which they are the only person, such as "the superintendent" or the "board president." The quote may express what the auditor found in many fewer words than the auditor would otherwise need.

- Quantitative terms have agreed-upon meaning as follows:

Descriptive Term	General Range Within the Group or Class Interviewed
Some or *a few*	Between two and five people determined by the overall size of the group
Many	More than 30% and less than a majority
A majority	no less than 50% and up to 75%
Most	75%–89%
Nearly all	90%–99%
All or *everyone*	100%

Adapted from audits sponsored by American Association of School Administrator's National Curriculum Audit Center.

Recommendation Headings

If the findings are done well, the recommendation headings will almost write themselves. There should not be very many. Even the largest, most troubled districts may have 10 or fewer recommendations. The auditor should present those recommendations that are the most important to improve the situation. Every recommendation should be directly tied to one or more findings.

A review of audits conducted in the last several years provided some of the following critical recommendations. In Exhibit 10.2.1, determine those standards to which the recommendation is related.

Exhibit 10.2.1

Activity: Recommendation Headings

Recommendation	Related Standard(s)
Coordinate administrative planning activities to provide for systematic curricular change.	
Establish and implement an instructional monitoring process to ensure effective curriculum and instructional practices.	
Revise and implement policies to attain educational equity.	
Design and implement a programmatic and participatory budgeting process.	
Develop, adopt, and implement a usable mission statement.	
Refine and enlarge the alternative education department to address inequities within the district.	
Implement a philosophy that accurately reflects the middle school concept.	
Establish a formal process for receiving and responding to district-generated reports.	

The Recommendation Narrative

The recommendation heading is typically supported with a paragraph that describes why such an action will benefit the district. The auditor then recommends specific actions to be taken. The first of these actions is related to the governance function, those things that the board of trustees needs to undertake. Governance functions typically use phrases or words like *charge administration, guide staff, serve as, request, confirm, support, identify,* and *monitor.* These are generally related to mission statements, policies, and direction to staff.

The second set of actions recommended concerns administrative functions, those activities with which the superintendent of the district would be involved. Administrative functions typically use phrases or words like *establish, formally institute, ensure that, clarify, require, publish, develop, assist, assign, oversee, report, encourage,* and *investigate.*

Recommendations are sequentially numbered. The specific activities within each recommendation are numbered sequentially with a G for governance functions and an A for administrative functions. For example:

Recommendation 1— Develop a comprehensive student assessment program that includes high-stakes exams.

G.1.1   the first action of Recommendation 1 for the board
G.1.2   the second action for the board
A.1.1   the first action of Recommendation 1 for the superintendent
A.1.2   the second action for the superintendent

This numbering system helps the staff organize the development of its action plan to address each recommendation.

The auditor needs to be sure that recommendations pass several tests. These include four of the tests for findings headings: recommendation statements must be unambiguous, accurate, important, and specific. In addition, they must be related to facts presented in the audit. If there has been no evidence that minority students are expelled in disproportionate numbers, there should be no finding directing the staff to improve the ratio of minority to nonminority students who are expelled. The auditor should be able to trace every recommendation to a finding.

Recommendations also must be reasonable and appropriate solutions to the situation. Schools cannot close for a year while the auditor's recommendations are enacted. Nonexistent funds cannot be used to fix buildings, develop curriculum, hire staff, expand the use of technology, or for any other desired improvement. Although some resources can be redirected to provide for the recommendations, everything will not come to a standstill while these activities are undertaken.

Discussion Questions

1. What was an experience you had receiving "good advice" as an insult?

2. What kinds of findings might do more harm than good?

3. Should an auditor omit a finding that will probably get an employee in trouble?

4. What truth is there to the belief that administrators can always find money for the things they want to do?

5. What would you consider the most important recommendation an auditor could make?

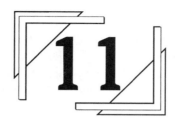

The Politics of Auditing

It is hard to imagine a sentence less eagerly heard than "It's time for your annual evaluation." Very few of us look forward to an honest appraisal of our work. Do we really know that what we are doing is flawless? Are we communicating our expectations for others clearly and giving them the support they need to meet their objectives? Are we 100% consistent and fair? Will we use information about our shortcomings to make real improvements? Are we managing all of our resources to be productive? It takes a brave person to ask for the truth, just as it takes a brave district to ask these same kinds of questions and seek honest answers.

Undertaking an Audit

Districts ask for audits for many reasons. If a new superintendent takes the leadership role, the district may be inclined to make a detailed analysis of the budget that would provide a multiyear road map for income and expenses. Perhaps the district is getting to know staff members and trying to form impressions about their strengths and weaknesses. Or it sees the buildings and identifies pressures for deferred maintenance, remodeling, and construction. When it comes to curriculum, however, all they can see are numerous problems with no obvious plan to address them, low test scores, accusations of waste, complaints about unmotivated students, high dropout rates, parent challenges to instructional materials, and an infinite list of frustrations, large and small.

Districts may ask for an audit because they have a court order to remediate equity issues. They need to create an overall plan that will help them establish control, clarify objectives, address infrastructure problems, use data to make decisions, and become a productive system for all students.

Some districts conduct audits because their low test scores incite the community to demand change. A district looks to the audit to pinpoint problems that are resulting from an assessment program that is not aligned with teaching and the written curriculum. It is interested in building on what it has to improve the learning opportunity for its students.

In some districts, the audit is a result of a staff person or board member learning about the audit process. This person sees the value in having a systematic, rational, well-thought-out analysis of the current curriculum management efforts. If the person is well placed in the organization, or can persuade someone who is, the audit can become a tool for building upon current strengths and addressing historic weaknesses.

Regardless of why the audit is conducted, it is a powerful tool for guiding change in a district. Even auditing just one of the five standards gives the district and school site staff critical elements to address. The more comprehensive the audit, the more valuable the resulting improvement plan.

The External Audit Team

Most audits have been done by a team of independent auditors. This team is usually comprised of a blend of colleagues from other districts, university professors who specialize in curriculum and educational administration, private consultants, graduate students, or other professionals who have been extensively trained to undertake the audit.

This outside team is formed just for the purpose of conducting a particular district's audit and is unlikely to ever form again. It will usually examine all five standards simultaneously as team members work together to share what they learn. Each member will have a specific standard on which to concentrate, but they also ask questions and make observations as needed by other team members.

As individuals, they blend with one another to provide complete expertise in the issues that face the district. If facilities are a serious problem, at least one team member will have specialized knowledge of construction, deferred maintenance, and facilities funding. If specially funded programs are a concern, team members will have expertise in federal, state, and foundation programs. Collectively, they will have the skill to systematically apply the elements of the audit and to identify unique strengths and weaknesses for the district.

The Internal Auditor

Although the process in this book is comparable to that of an external audit, its real focus is on the internal auditor. It provides guidance through the concrete steps to be followed in a standardized format that is likely to lead anyone who follows the steps carefully to the same conclusions about the district's curriculum management.

Some districts prefer to have the audit conducted by one or more staff persons. This may be a newcomer who brings no known agenda to the process. It may be the district historian who knows the operational ins and outs of the last several decades. It may be a small group of district office staff who are especially interested in curriculum. It may be staff members who are working on their graduate degrees and need a worthy project.

The internal auditor might initially examine only one of the five standards. Subsequent standards may be audited as the recommendations are implemented.

The internal auditor is expected to bring an objective eye to the process, to maintain confidences offered by colleagues, and to look toward the long-term good of the district. The internal auditor may feel pressure to highlight certain flaws or gloss over others if his or her supervisor has an agenda. However, the internal audit can be a successful approach if the auditor is free to undertake the process openly and honestly.

Auditor as Critic

Typical relationships between district staff and financial auditors are characterized by fear. The staff does not announce the problems they know exist, and they hope to hide any that are uncovered from supervisors or funding agencies. Only when the auditor and staff have developed a relationship of trust and mutual respect can the audit process promote accountability and improvement.

Relationships between district staff and curriculum management auditors are similar to those. The auditor is not always welcomed with an open embrace. If the audit has been requested without the support of the superintendent, it will be perceived as a career stopper. Some staff will clam up and others will openly take shots and rid themselves of years of hostility and petty grudges. If the audit has been requested by the community without the understanding of the staff, it is likely to be greeted with a hard sell in which most interviewees brag and boast without addressing the areas that most concern them.

An auditor who is skilled, however, will get past the perception that the auditor's role is that of critic. Many staff members have greeted the auditor with enthusiasm—excited about the good things that are being done in the district and making clear statements to express the need for improvement. In the formal and informal exchange that characterizes the auditor's work, staff members can provide numerous suggestions that add to the power of the recommendations.

Discussion Questions

1. What might a district hope to achieve from an audit?
2. What risks could a district take by inviting an external team to audit?
3. What risks could an employee take by conducting an internal audit?
4. What are the advantages of external audits? Internal audits?
5. What are the differences between a curriculum management audit and a financial audit?

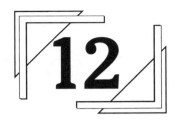

Scenario: After the Audit

Sally Jamison is a new teacher who has recently graduated from the state college near her hometown. After several months of searching, she has just been offered her first job. She looks forward to her assignment with a mixture of enthusiasm and fear. She had heard some negative things about the district, but her recent inquiries seemed promising. Several of the subjects she will be teaching really excite her, and she has many ideas about how to share her excitement with her students. But some of the units she expects to teach puzzle her, and she is unclear about how to present the information.

She is particularly worried because of all the talk going around about "accountability" and "getting rid of teachers who don't perform." She prepares a list of questions, but its length begins to scare her as she worries that the initial impression she will make is one of a teacher who has no clue about what to do.

Sally, however, is lucky. Four years ago, her district completed a curriculum management audit. It implemented the recommendations of the audit team and is prepared to support Sally with the help she needs.

Sally's first stop is her new school. The principal, a veteran administrator and instructional leader, welcomes her enthusiastically and sets the tone. This is a place where children are cared about, standards are high, and expectations are clear. The principal hands Sally a set of documents: the board-adopted instructional focus, the current curriculum guides for the core courses she will teach, a map, and a directory of site and district staff. Sally also receives contact information for the teacher who has been assigned to mentor her and a calendar of teacher activities. Clutching her new key nervously but proudly, she searches for her classroom.

Room 7 is well lit and well maintained despite its age. The bulletin boards are empty but a cabinet contains the art supplies she needs to fill them with engaging and attractive lessons. The furniture includes a combination of individual desks and tables with chairs. Part of the room is carpeted; part of it is tiled. Off the back door is a grassy area with some bare ground to use as a garden.

Sally quickly peruses the curriculum guide. She is relieved to find objectives, timelines, resources, tests, sample lessons, and nearly everything else she can imagine needing. The filing cabinet reveals folders of lesson ideas coded to the objectives she saw in the guides. Some of the patterns and materials she needs are there, too. As she is looking around the room at the shelves of texts and library books, she hears a rapping at the door. Pat, her mentor, has arrived and with one quick, reassuring smile, Sally knows this is someone who will support rather than judge her.

Pat tells Sally about the children she will soon meet. Even though most of the children speak at least some English, many of them do not yet read well enough to understand the social studies materials and will need other strategies. Pat tells Sally about the upcoming teacher trainings in literacy and working with limited-English-proficient students. Sally remembers her education professor's advice not take on too much at once. Adjusting to her new profession will take some time.

With Pat's support and phone number, Sally feels ready for her district office orientation. She is impressed by the large facility that displays student work along the hallways. But she is not prepared for the impression the district will make when she enters the conference room where the orientation is held. The superintendent personally greets her by name and introduces her to the key staff. Finance, education services, personnel, facilities—the names fly past her but the message is clear. She is important and appreciated.

The superintendent's opening remarks state the mission: We increase student achievement in a safe, positive environment to prepare students for the 21st century. This message is echoed by the following speakers and Sally notices it on the letterhead, on her contract, on her business cards, on the conference room wall and on nearly every other surface she sees. "This district lives its mission," says the superintendent. It guides how money is spent, what conferences the staff will attend, how decisions are made, what role parents play, how the community is involved, what positions employees hold—every aspect of the district is governed by the mission.

The board president is introduced. She echoes the commitment to this mission and further defines the current focus for student achievement: All students will read proficiently by third grade, use technology as tools to support learning at all levels, and meet the expectations established for each subject. Sally notices these expectations in her packet and is relieved to realize they are included in the objectives she saw in her curriculum guide.

The assessment director speaks next. This is the part Sally dreads—being held responsible for how students do on a test she has never seen. Although she does not understand all of the director's presentation, she gets the message: Accountability is important and that includes providing the support teachers need to do well. There will be follow-up sessions on assessment so that Sally can become comfortable with terms such as *normal curve equivalent* and *stanine* that are used to monitor changes in achievement level. The director's handout lists the key things that students need to know for the test. Again, this list parallels the board president's expectations and the objectives in the curriculum guide. Sally notes the time and date for the next session in her new planning book.

Secretly, Sally is relieved as her first day in the new district ends. It was not what she had expected. The rumors she had heard and the checking up she had done while searching for a job had given her a different image. She had expected general chaos. She had not expected the positive attitude and coordinated support she received.

Had Sally been new to the district 5 years earlier, she would have found more truth to these rumors. The district had been in disarray. Parents were dissatisfied with the test scores, buildings were poorly maintained, there were charges of fiscal mismanagement, and the turnover rate among teachers was high. The board's frustration had prompted the superintendent to present an aggressive solution: a curriculum management audit. As a result of the audit, the district had a set of findings that provided a road map to attain high standards, had specific recommendations to follow, and had a coordinated commitment to school improvement. Sally, all of her colleagues, and the students of the district, are now benefiting from the results of the curriculum management audit.

Glossary of Key Audit Terms

Accountability: The process of holding and being held to previously defined and measured expectations.

Alignment: Matching the written, taught, and tested curricula.

Articulation: Communicating and planning so that lessons will build on each other as students proceed from one grade to the next.

Assessment: Gathering and using information to make informed decisions about students and instructional strategies; may include norm-referenced tests, criterion-referenced tests, portfolios, and other forms of data collection.

Audit: An objective measurement of an agreed-upon standard; the report that provides information about that measurement.

Chain of command: The hierarchy of relationships in an organization, usually based on who has the greatest array of responsibilities to who has the least.

Congruity: The degree to which components match; for example, in triangulation the goal is to have the written, tested, and taught curriculum match each to produce congruity.

Coordination: Communicating and planning so that lessons will build on each other as students proceed across subjects and schools in the same grade.

Data sources: The elements of triangulation: interviews, documents, and visitations.

Disaggregation: Components of data that can be broken into discrete parts; for example, language arts norm-referenced test scores by grade, gender, ethnicity, and mobility factor.

Equality: Allocating resources in equal amounts; for example, providing $25 per pupil for textbooks.

Equity: Allocating resources as needed to produce equal results; for example, providing $10 per pupil, per grade below reading level, for textbooks.

Finding: A statement of fact about the condition being measured; the finding is the organizer in the audit.

Institutionalization: A practice is institutionalized when it becomes an ongoing part of the organization without outside finding or legislation.

Intervention: Any instructional strategy used to affect the results.

Logical grouping of functions: Displaying similar jobs on the organization chart; for example, putting all administrative services together, separate from educational services.

Predictability: Having data that is dependable and comprehensive enough to determine what is likely to happen next.

Promising practice: Experiments, interventions, and risks that seem likely to produce positive changes.

Rationality: Being goal driven; a rational organization adheres to a clearly stated mission.

Recommendation: An informed suggestion for improvement based on a documented finding.

Span of control: The number of people and functions being supervised by one individual.

Standards: Agreed-upon goals against which quality is measured; the curriculum management audit has five standards.

Table of organization (T/O): An organizational chart.

Triangulation: The audit process used to develop findings based on corroborating information gathered from interviews, documents, and visitations.

References

Des Dixon, R. G. (1994, January). Future schools and how to get there from here. *Phi Delta Kappan*, 360-365.

Doyle, D. (1992, March). The challenge, the opportunity. *Phi Delta Kappan*, 512-520.

English, F. W. (1988). *Curriculum auditing*. Lancaster, PA: Technomic.

English, F. W. (1992) *Deciding what to teach and test: Developing, aligning, and auditing the curriculum*. Newbury Park, CA: Corwin.

Ferrell, K. (1992, June). Some direction for our schools. *Omni*, p. 8.

Frase, L. E., English, F. E., & Poston, W. K. (1995). *The curriculum management audit: Improving school quality*. Lancaster, PA: Technomic.

National Commission on Excellence in Education. (1983). *A nation at risk*. Washington, DC: U.S. Department of Education.

Shanker, A. (1990, January). The end of the traditional model of schooling— and a proposal for using incentives to restructure our schools. *Phi Delta Kappan*, 345.

CORWIN
PRESS

The Corwin Press logo—a raven striding across an open book—represents the happy union of courage and learning. We are a professional-level publisher of books and journals for K-12 educators, and we are committed to creating and providing resources that embody these qualities. Corwin's motto is "Success for All Learners."